• HBJ READING P

CELEBRATIONS

LAUREATE EDITION

LEVEL 8

Bernice E. Cullinan
Roger C. Farr
W. Dorsey Hammond
Nancy L. Roser
Dorothy S. Strickland

HBJ **HARCOURT BRACE JOVANOVICH, PUBLISHERS**
Orlando   San Diego   Chicago   Dallas

Acknowledgments

For permission to reprint copyrighted material, grateful acknowledgment is made to the following sources:

Atheneum Publishers, a division of Macmillan, Inc.: Adapted from *The Miser Who Wanted the Sun* by Jurg Obrist. Copyright © 1983 by Artemis Verlag/Zurich & Munich; English translation copyright © 1983 by Methuen Children's Books Ltd. A Margaret K. McElderry book.

Eleanor Clymer: From *The Spider, The Cave and the Pottery Bowl* (Titled: "The Cave") by Eleanor Clymer. Published by Atheneum Publishers, Inc., 1971.

Coward, McCann & Geoghegan: Adapted from *The Desert: What Lives There* by Andrew Bronin. Text copyright © 1972 by Andrew Bronin.

Dodd, Mead & Company, Inc.: From *The Buried Treasure*, retold by Djemma Bider. Copyright © 1982 by Djemma Bider.

Dover Publications, Inc.: "The Corn-Grinding Song," a poem of the Zuñi Indians from *The Indians' Book*, edited by Natalie Curtis. Published by Dover Publications, Inc., New York, 1968.

E. P. Dutton, a division of NAL Penguin Inc.: Adapted from "The Case of the Cave Drawings" in *Encyclopedia Brown Keeps the Peace* by Donald J. Sobol. Copyright © 1969 by Donald J. Sobol. A Lodestar book.

E. P. Dutton, a division of NAL Penguin Inc. and the Canadian Publishers, McClelland and Stewart, Toronto: "Wind on the Hill" from *Now We Are Six* by A. A. Milne. Copyright 1927 by E. P. Dutton, renewed 1955 by A. A. Milne.

Lydia Freeman: From *Hattie the Backstage Bat*, story and pictures by Don Freeman. Copyright © 1970 by Don Freeman. Published by Viking Penguin Inc.

Harcourt Brace Jovanovich, Inc.: From p. 172 in *HBJ Science*, Level Green by Elizabeth K. Cooper et al. Cover illustrations from *Big Anthony and the Magic Ring; The Prince of the Dolomites;* and *Strega Nona's Magic Lessons.* Copyright © 1979, 1980, 1982 by Tomie dePaola. Title page illustration and cover illustration from *Sing, Pierrot, Sing* by Tomie dePaola. Copyright © 1983 by Tomie dePaola.

Harper & Row, Publishers, Inc.: Abridged and adapted from Chapter 3 of *Bicycle Rider* by Mary Scioscia. Copyright © 1983 by Mary Scioscia.

Houghton Mifflin Company: Adapted from *Encore for Eleanor*, written and illustrated by Bill Peet. Copyright © 1981 by William B. Peet. Adapted from *Merle, the High-Flying Squirrel*, written and illustrated by Bill Peet. Copyright © 1974 by William B. Peet.

The Instructor Publications, Inc., New York, NY 10017: "The Wheel" by Josephine Van Dolzen Pease and "The Spider Web" by Truda McCoy from *Poetry Place Anthology.* Copyright © 1983 by The Instructor Publications, Inc.

Little, Brown and Company: Adapted from "Why Spider Lives in Ceilings" in *The Adventures of Spider*, retold by Joyce Cooper Arkhurst. Copyright © 1964 by Joyce Cooper Arkhurst.

Little, Brown and Company, in association with The Atlantic Monthly Press: Adapted from *All Except Sammy* by Gladys Yessayan Cretan. Text copyright © 1966 by Gladys Yessayan Cretan.

Lothrop, Lee & Shepard Books, a division of William Morrow & Company, Inc.: Abridged and adapted from *The Great Town and Country Bicycle Balloon Chase* (Titled: "The Bicycle Balloon Chase") by Barbara Douglass. Copyright © 1984 by Barbara Douglass. Illustrations from pp. 2–3, 8, 21 and 25 by Carol Newsom. Copyright © 1984 by Carol Newsom. Entire text, and illustrations from pp. 5, 10, 16, 24–25, and 32 in *Sam Johnson and the Blue Ribbon Quilt*, written and illustrated by Lisa Campbell Ernst. Copyright © 1983 by Lisa Campbell Ernst.

Macmillan Publishing Company: "Learning About Bar Graphs" from pp. 58–59 in *Communities, People and Places* by John Jarolimek, Senior Author, and Ruth Pelz. Copyright © 1985 by Macmillan Publishing Company, a division of Macmillan, Inc.

Margaret Mahy: From *The Dragon of an Ordinary Family* by Margaret Mahy. Text © 1969 by Franklin Watts, Inc. Published in the United States by Franklin Watts, Inc. and in Great Britain by William Heinemann Ltd.

McGraw-Hill Book Company: From pp. 115–117 and 138 in *Gateways to Science*, Book 3, by Neal J. Holmes et al. Copyright © 1983 by McGraw-Hill, Inc.

McIntosh and Otis, Inc.: From *Pornada* by Mary Francis Shura. Copyright © 1968 by Mary Francis Shura. Published by Atheneum Publishers, Inc.

Methuen & Co. Ltd.: "The Paint Box" from *The Flattered Flying Fish and Other Poems* by E. V. Rieu.

Methuen Children's Books Ltd.: Abridged and adapted from *Hilda the Hen Who Wouldn't Give Up* by Jill Tomlinson.

G. P. Putnam's Sons: Adapted from *Now One Foot, Now the Other*, written and illustrated by Tomie dePaola. Copyright © 1981 by Tomie dePaola. Cover illustration from *The Legend of the Bluebonnet*, retold and illustrated by Tomie dePaola. Copyright © 1983 by Tomie dePaola. Cover illustration from *The Knight and the Dragon*, written and illustrated by Tomie dePaola. Copyright © 1980 by Tomie dePaola.

Random House, Inc.: "Alphabet Stew" by Jack Prelutsky from *The Random House Book of Poetry for Children*, selected by Jack Prelutsky. Copyright © 1983 by Random House, Inc.

Marian Reiner on behalf of Eve Merriam: "Shh" from *A Word or Two With You* by Eve Merriam. Copyright © 1981 by Eve Merriam. All rights reserved.

Scott, Foresman and Company: From p. 229 in *City, Town, and Country* by Dr. Joan Schreiber et al. Copyright © 1983 by Scott, Foresman and Company.

Silver Burdett Company: From *The World and Its People: Communities and Resources* by Richard H. Loftin. © 1984 by Silver Burdett Company.

The Literary Trustees of Walter de la Mare and The Society of Authors as their representative: "Seeds" by Walter de la Mare.

Yoshiko Uchida: From pp. 15–38 in *Sumi's Special Happening* by Yoshiko Uchida. Published by Charles Scribner's Sons, 1966.

Albert Whitman & Company: From *Words in Our Hands* by Ada B. Litchfield. Text © 1980 by Ada B. Litchfield.

Contents

Unit 2
Landscapes

Unit 3
Applause

Unit 4
Windows

Me and Neesie *by Eloise Greenfield. Crowell.* Janell has her own made-up friend to keep her company and to make mischief with until she can go to school.

The Great Race of the Birds and Animals *by Paul Goble. Bradbury.* In a legend of the Cheyenne and Sioux Indians, power over the buffaloes is won through a great race.

Little Pig and the Blue-Green Sea *by Tannis Vernon. Crown.* Little Pig escapes during a trip to market. His dream comes true when he becomes the ship's mascot.

Hot-Air Henry *by Mary Calhoun. Morrow.* A cat stows away on a hot-air balloon and ends up having the adventure of its life.

Jed and the Space Bandits *by Jean Marzollo and Claudio Marzollo. Dial.* Jed and his teddy bear robot have different adventures while they are on space patrol.

Children's Choices Author

What happens to Merle as he travels out West? What does he find when he gets there?

Merle the High-Flying Squirrel

story and pictures by Bill Peet

Merle was a shy little squirrel who lived in a big city park up in an oak tree. He hardly ever came down out of the tree. The noisy traffic and the tall gray buildings scared him. Even the people who came to the park frightened him.

"I'm tired of being scared," Merle said one morning. "It's no fun at all. From now on, I'm going to try and be brave enough to take a trip somewhere. I might go all the way across the park and back."

That same morning, Merle heard some people talking about all the places they had been and all the things they had seen.

"I've seen a lot of things," said one man. "However, nothing ever got me like the big trees out in the West. Why, some of them shoot up as tall as the tallest building. When you are standing there, you feel mighty small, not just small like here in the city. It's a good feeling. There's a great quietness about them. You've got to see them to understand what I mean."

After the people had gone, Merle sat up in the oak trying to picture a tree as tall as a building. "I just can't believe it," he said. "Not until I see one. So I must take a trip out West, but I don't dare run along the roads. The only safe way for a squirrel to travel is on the telephone wires."

So, with a sad "good-bye" to his oak tree, Merle took a flying leap over to the nearest telephone wire.

Then after making sure which way was west, he started off. High-wire walking was something new for Merle. He was not too steady at first. The noise of the traffic down below gave him the shakes.

"Remember," he said, "no more being scared. I've got to be brave! Brave!" Just like that, Merle got over the shakes. Soon he was running along the wires at a fast, steady clip.

"At this rate," he said, "the trip out West will be easy. I'll be there in a flash!"

Before he knew it, however, most of the day was gone. It was late afternoon and he was still in the city. Finally, Merle hopped to the top of a telephone pole to catch his breath and give his feet a rest. Suddenly he realized the trip was going to be too hard.

Merle sighed, "It is way too much of a trip for a squirrel. It would take forever."

So Merle gave up his dream of seeing the big trees and headed back for the park. By now, the sun was setting. It would be dark long before he reached the oak tree. So Merle began looking around for a safe place to spend the night.

Pretty soon he saw a big sign on the roof of a tall building. In one leap, he was on the roof. Then, picking out a huge letter S, Merle curled up in the bottom of the letter and fell sound asleep.

The next morning, Merle woke up to the sound of voices coming from somewhere below. He sat up with a shiver of fright.

"We could grab it by the tail," someone said, "if we could reach it."

In a flash, Merle was on top of the letter S. Looking down at the street, he spotted two boys, but they were not looking up at him. They were staring up at a kite tangled in the telephone wires.

"We had better get someone to help us," said one boy. "Let's go!"

As the boys raced away to get help, Merle had a bright idea. "I'll surprise them," he said. "I'll untangle the tail and have the kite down before they get back."

Then Merle hurried out onto the wires and set to work. He was so busy tugging at the tangle, he didn't notice the storm clouds rolling over the city. A fierce wind came up so quickly that Merle was caught by surprise.

Swoosh! The kite was swept off the wires with Merle clinging tightly to the tail. Suddenly he was sailing high over the buildings up into the black clouds. Now he was *really* scared.

Merle was afraid the kite might be ripped to pieces, and then down he would tumble into a street full of traffic. The boys had made a good, strong kite, however, and it sailed lightly along in the middle of the fierce storm.

For a second, there was a break in the clouds. Merle caught sight of the earth far below with a tiny speck of a house here and there. "I must be a mile high," thought Merle. "I'm on a flying trip, and it might be a long one if I can just hang on." He tightened his hold on the fast-moving tail.

At last, the fierce storm blew itself out. The wind died down to a whisper, and the kite dropped out of the clouds. The tail stopped moving and Merle found himself drifting down. All he could see below him were rocks and dry brush. There was no sign of a tree anywhere.

"No!" cried Merle, "not here! I couldn't stand to live here, not even for a day!"

Just as the kite was about to touch the ground, along came a whirlwind, swirling up clouds of dust. It caught the kite, and Merle was taken for another ride.

Then a powerful crosswind sent the kite sailing over high mountain peaks. "We've gone far enough," begged Merle, pulling at the kite tail. "Come down, you silly old kite!"

However, the kite kept sailing for hours, carried along by a lively breeze high over more mountain peaks and more forests.

Just before sunset, the kite began drifting down through rosy pink clouds. Merle noticed the kite was heading straight for the sea! He realized he had made the trip too far out West. "I'm done for," Merle groaned.

All at once, the kite stopped with a jerk. The tail had caught onto the tip of a runt of a pine tree. Merle hopped onto a branch for a look around.

Thick fog covered the ground. Here and there Merle saw a runt of a pine tree. "What a strange place," said Merle. "At least I'm lucky to have landed in a tree and not in the sea. Even if it is just a runt of a tree, it's a place to sleep."

When Merle woke up the next morning, he was
so surprised he nearly tumbled off the branch.
What a tumble it would have been! The fog had
drifted away and Merle discovered he was high
in the air, up in the very tip top of a huge
redwood! On every side were more huge trees!
He saw a whole forest of them!

"I can't believe it," cried Merle, "I'm here! I'm
way out West in the big trees! They *are* as tall as
buildings and a whole lot more beautiful. There
is a great quietness about them. I feel mighty
small out here, but not as small as I did in the
city. It is a good feeling!"

1. What did Merle find when he got out West?

2. What four things did Merle see through the clouds as he traveled West?

3. How did Merle's dream finally come true?

4. What clue in the story made you realize that Merle thought the boys wanted to grab his tail?

5. Do you think that Merle was a lucky squirrel? Why?

6. Merle's dream was to go out West. What fears did he have to overcome to make his dream come true?

Think and Write

Prewrite

Merle had quite an adventure! Make a list of as many things as you can remember about Merle's adventure out West and about how he felt during his journey.

Kites that Helped with Work

Did you know that people began flying kites over two thousand years ago? The Chinese were the first people to invent and use kites. The kites they made were very beautiful. Some were shaped like fish, while others were made to look like dragons.

Sometimes the Chinese people flew kites just for fun. At other times they used kites to help them with their work. They tied a fishing line to the end of a kite. When a fish bit the bait, the kite moved. Then the kite and the fish were pulled in. Chinese farmers put kites in their fields to scare away birds that tried to eat their crops.

Parts of a Kite

Most kites have three main parts: a frame, a cover, and a flying line. The frame may be made of wood or plastic sticks. The cover is usually made of paper, plastic, silk, or nylon. These materials are used because they are so light. Thin nylon string, which can be wrapped around a stick, is used for the flying line.

A tail is used to stop a kite from spinning on a windy day. The tails may be made of cloth, paper, or feathers. The larger a kite is, the bigger its tail needs to be.

Famous People Who Flew Kites

Many famous people have flown kites. In 1752, Benjamin Franklin discovered electricity by flying a kite. The Wright brothers learned a lot about flying by watching box kites. This helped them to build their first airplane. Alexander Graham Bell, the inventor of the telephone, also flew kites. In 1907, he built a box kite that lifted a man 168 feet into the air! The man stayed up for seven minutes.

Today almost all kites are flown for fun. The next time you fly a kite, remember that you are doing something that people have been doing for thousands of years.

1. What kinds of kites are described in the selection?

2. How did the Chinese use kites?

3. What famous people flew kites?

4. Do you think you would like to fly a kite? Why?

5. Where in the story does it tell you that many different materials can be used to make kites?

6. Why should we be happy that Benjamin Franklin and the Wright brothers were kite flyers?

Prewrite

Choose one of the following activities.

1. Fold a piece of paper to look like a kite. On your kite, use different colors to write some of the words that describe what it might be like to be a kite and fly over the ...h.

2. Think about a kite that you might like to have. What color would it be? How would it be shaped? What kind of tail would it have? Now, draw a big picture of it.

Draft

1. If you picked number 1, use some of the words you have written to create a poem in the shape of a kite. Your poem should help the reader to feel what it might be like to be a kite.

2. If you have drawn a picture of your "dream" kite, write a story about the kind of kite you might like to have.

Revise

First, read your poem or your story to a friend. Then let your friend read it back to you. Did you share all the feelings and ideas you wanted to? Let your friend help you find ways to make it say all that you want it to say. Make the changes you need to make.

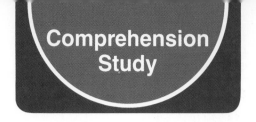

Summarize

A **summary** of a story is putting an author's story into your own words. When you **summarize** a story, you must tell enough so that the author's story will be understood. You must choose the most important parts to tell, but you don't give every detail.

Read Melissa's summary of the story, *Merle, the High-Flying Squirrel.*

> Merle was a shy city squirrel who was frightened by the traffic. He wanted to go out West to see the redwood trees. He rode on a kite blown by some storms. After many adventures, he finally landed in a redwood tree in the West. His dream had come true.

Melissa's summary would help you understand the story about Merle. She has told the important parts of the story. She has left out details that are not as important.

Read these summaries of *Kites in Flight*. Decide which one tells only important parts of the article and which one includes details that are not important.

A. Kites can be made in all shapes and sizes. Some kites have long tails with bits of colored glass attached. Brightly-colored kites can stand out against the blue sky.

B. People have been flying kites for thousands of years. Long ago, some people used kites to help them with their work. Now kites are flown mostly for fun.

Summary A includes too many details. It is not useful for someone who wants to know the important parts of the article. All parts of Summary B are important. Summary B would help you think about the most important ideas in *Kites in Flight*.

As you read, it is helpful to stop sometimes and summarize the story or article in your mind. A good summary will help you understand and better remember what you have read.

How does a bicycle race become an exciting voyage for both Gina and her grandfather?

The Bicycle Balloon Chase

by Barbara Douglass

"What does that mean?" Gina asked Grandpa, pointing to the poster. It was the third poster she'd seen that week. "What's a bicycle balloon chase?"

The man in the bike shop told them about it. "A big hot-air balloon will take off from the park this Saturday. Only the wind knows which way it will go. We'll follow it on our bikes. After the balloon lands, the first two bikers who get close enough to touch it will win a free ride in it."

After breakfast each day, Gina and Grandpa pedaled all over town. They rode uphill on Main Street. They rode downhill on Maple Street. Gina counted five more posters. Grandpa counted shortcuts.

"Only the wind knows which way the balloon will go," he said. "So we have to know the shortest way to everywhere."

On Saturday Gina and Grandpa were up before sunrise. After breakfast Gina packed apples and peanuts while Grandpa pumped air into their bicycle tires. At last Grandpa put on his cap and said, "I do believe we're ready. Let's go chase that balloon."

In the park Gina saw bicycles with great big front wheels and little tiny back wheels. She saw bicycles with two seats and four pedals. She even saw something with only one wheel, called a unicycle, but she didn't see a balloon.

Gina saw a woman with a parrot and a basket in the back of a pickup truck. "Where's the balloon?" asked Gina.

"Look in the back of that truck," Grandpa told her. "The woman is an aeronaut, the basket is a gondola, and the balloon is in that bag."

"I thought it was a *big* balloon," said Gina.

"It will be," said Grandpa. "Wait and see."

Gina waited. The aeronaut and her helpers unloaded the truck. They set the gondola on the grass and tipped it over. They opened the bag and pulled out a bundle of green, red, purple, and blue material, and they unrolled it and unrolled it.

The long, skinny bundle had a big mouth. Helpers held it open. The aeronaut turned on a fan. The bundle began to stretch.

Then the aeronaut turned on a burner. The balloon began to fill with air. Finally it stood up straight and tall. It was taller than ten buildings stacked one on top of another.

"Ready?" called the aeronaut.

"Ready!" answered the bikers.

The helpers let go of the ropes. The balloon floated up and away.

A man on a bicycle with a big front wheel said, "I think the wind will blow the balloon this way. Let's take Main Street."

A woman on a unicycle said, "I think the wind will blow the balloon this way. Let's take Maple Street."

A man and a woman on a bicycle built for two said, "This way," and "That way," both at once. They took a spill. Grandpa took a shortcut. Gina followed Grandpa.

When the balloon drifted this way, Grandpa took this shortcut. When the balloon drifted that way, Grandpa took that shortcut. Gina followed Grandpa through every shortcut in town.

The balloon drifted into the country. It led them past a dairy, a farm, and a ranch. There it drifted even lower. "Hurry, hurry," said Gina to Grandpa. "I think we might be first!"

Grandpa and Gina pedaled faster. When the balloon dipped down, they were ready to run to it. Then the aeronaut called, "Whoops! A bull! We'll have to look for a better place."

The burner hissed. The bull roared. The parrot squawked in fright. The aeronaut called, "Oh, no! Gypsy! You come back here!"

The parrot flew this way. The balloon blew that way. Gina followed the squawking parrot. Grandpa followed Gina. All the other bikers followed the balloon.

The parrot didn't take any shortcuts. It led them back past the ranch, all the way around the farm, and across the dairy before it landed on a giant sunflower. Gina climbed up and caught it.

Quickly, Gina and Grandpa turned their bikes around. They pedaled harder and faster than ever past the dairy and the farm and the ranch.

They were the last ones to reach the balloon. The winners were ready to take their ride. The burner hissed, and the balloon tugged at the ropes.

Suddenly the aeronaut called to her helpers, "Wait! Don't let go yet."

She pointed to Gina and Grandpa and said, "Please put your bicycles in the back of our chase truck and come over here."

They did. The aeronaut said, "There's room in the gondola for two more bikers. Anyone who is smart enough to catch my runaway parrot should have a chance to go up in my balloon. Welcome aboard!"

1. In what way was the bicycle balloon chase exciting for Gina and Grandpa?

2. What is a bicycle balloon chase?

3. Why were Gina and Grandpa the last ones to reach the balloon?

4. What did you think when Gina and Grandpa followed the parrot and not the balloon?

5. When did you realize that Gina and Grandpa were going to get a ride in the balloon?

6. Gina and Grandpa helped the aeronaut by catching her parrot. How did that help them, too?

Think and Write

Prewrite

Think about the bicycle balloon chase. Imagine that you and your friend are entering the balloon chase with Gina and her Grandpa. What might happen to change the middle or ending of the story? Share with your classmate how you might change the middle or ending of this story. Then listen as your classmate tells you his or her middle or ending.

Copy and complete the chart below.

Beginning	Middle	End
My friend and I entered a balloon chase.	We got lost during the race.	▬▬▬▬▬
▬▬▬▬▬	▬▬▬▬▬	▬▬▬▬▬
▬▬▬▬▬	▬▬▬▬▬	▬▬▬▬▬

Draft

Now, write a story with a different middle or ending. Remember to include yourself and a friend in your story.

Revise

Read your story to a classmate. Then have your classmate tell you the beginning, middle, and ending of your story. Discuss what needs to be changed to improve your story.

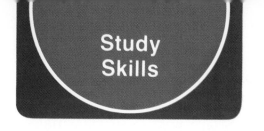
Diagrams

Diagram of a Hot-air Balloon

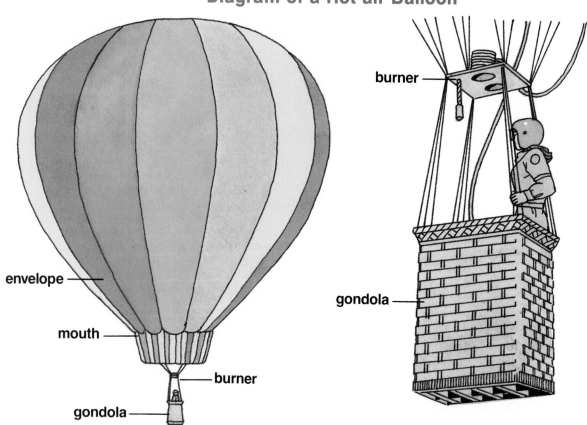

envelope

mouth

burner

gondola

burner

gondola

A **diagram** is a drawing used to explain how something is put together or how it works. Some diagrams have titles. The title of this diagram is "Diagram of a Hot-air Balloon." All diagrams have labels. Labels name the important parts of a diagram. They are connected by lines to the parts they name. What are the labels on this diagram? Did you answer *envelope, mouth, burner,* and *gondola?*

A diagram may have an **inset.** The inset shows details about one part of the diagram.

Look at the diagram on page 36. What is the largest part of the hot-air balloon? Yes, the envelope is the largest part. Notice that a line connects that part of the drawing with its label, *envelope.*

Now find the labels *burner* and *mouth* on the diagram. The burner heats the air by burning gas and making a flame. The mouth is the opening to the envelope. The air enters the balloon through the mouth. The envelope rises and floats high above the ground when the air in the envelope is heated.

Look at the diagram. In which part of the hot-air balloon can people ride? Yes, people can ride in the gondola. How did you know? You can tell because a person is shown in the gondola on the diagram.

By using the diagram, you have learned about the main parts of a balloon. You have a better idea of how a hot-air balloon works.

Textbook Application:
Diagrams in Science

    Diagrams are often used in textbooks. They are used to make something easier to understand. Look at the diagram of a bicycle below. What is the title? Study the labels. What parts of the bicycle have been labeled? Now read the paragraphs on page 39. They will explain how the labeled parts of the bicycle work.

Diagram of a Bicycle

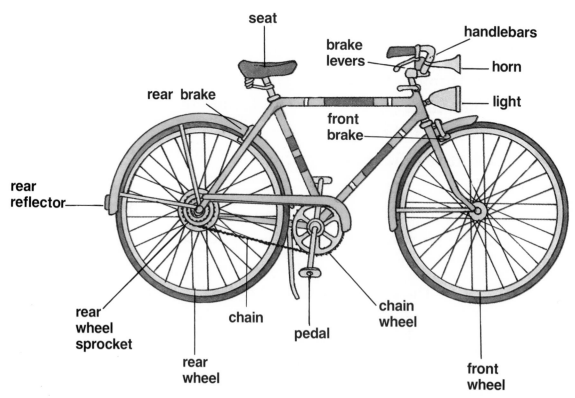

seat

brake levers

handlebars

horn

rear brake

light

front brake

rear reflector

rear wheel sprocket

chain

pedal

chain wheel

rear wheel

front wheel

A bicycle has many parts. Some of them are the seat, the pedals, and the handlebars. Some safety parts are the brakes, a horn or bell, lights, and a reflector. The brakes help the bicycle stop. The reflector makes a bicycle easier to see at night.

A rider pushes the pedals up and down. The pedals are attached to a wheel called a chain wheel. The chain wheel has teeth on it. The pedals make the chain wheel go around. The chain wheel is attached by a chain to the rear-wheel sprocket. The chain moves when the chain wheel moves. The chain makes the rear-wheel sprocket turn. When the rear-wheel sprocket turns, the bicycle goes forward.

—*Gateways to Science*, McGraw-Hill

The diagram makes it easier for you to understand how a bicycle works. Having a picture of the important parts of a bicycle helps you understand the paragraph. Diagrams are useful for understanding how things work or how things are put together.

This selection is from a book about Marshall Taylor. Find out how a bicycle race changed his life.

Bicycle Rider

by Mary Scioscia

About a hundred years ago, a boy named Marshall Taylor got his first job in Mr. Hay's bicycle shop. There was a big bicycle race in Indianapolis each year. On the day of the big race, Mr. Hay asked Marshall to help him sell bicycles at the bicycle track.

As this true story begins, Marshall is watching excitedly while more than a hundred bicycle racers gather near the starting line.

"Attention everyone! All those in the first one-mile race line up at the starting line," a loud voice called.

"First one-mile race?" asked Marshall. "How many races will there be?"

"There will be several one-mile races before the main ten-mile race," said Mr. Hay. "Marshall, you just gave me an idea. You should ride in one of the one-mile races. I'll ask the judges if you can," said Mr. Hay.

When Mr. Hay came back, he said, "You can ride in the next one-mile race. Pick any of the bikes we brought."

At the starting line, Mr. Hay said, "Each time around the track is one lap. Five laps make a mile. Don't worry if you forget how many laps you've gone. When you hear the bell ring, you will know it is the bell lap. That means one lap left to go for the mile."

Marshall got on the bicycle and clipped his feet onto the pedals. A tall, thin boy in a red shirt got in line next to Marshall.

All the racers leaned over their handlebars. Their helpers held the bicycles steady. The starter raised his starting gun. "One! Two! Three!" the starter shouted. *Bang!*

Mr. Hay gave Marshall a strong push. He shot ahead. A tall boy got ahead of Marshall. Four more people got ahead. Marshall rode past one of them. He pushed his legs as hard as he could.

Around and around the racers went. Now there were seven people ahead of Marshall. *Ding, ding, ding,* the bell rang. Marshall knew that there was one more lap to go for the mile.

Marshall speeded up. One racer crossed the finish line . . . two more . . . another. Next was the boy in the red shirt. Right after him came the tall boy. Then Marshall crossed the line. Mr. Hay hurried over to help him stop.

"You came in number seven. That's great!" said Mr. Hay.

"It wasn't very good," said Marshall. "Six people beat me."

"You beat over forty people. You've never been in a race before. You're good enough to try the ten-mile race."

"Oh, no," said Marshall. "I could never win that."

"No," said Mr. Hay. "You couldn't win, but I think you could finish. Try it, Marshall. If you get tired, just stop. Many racers will drop out before the fifty laps are done."

During the last one-mile race, Mr. Hay spoke to the judges again. Marshall rested with several other riders in the middle of the track.

"Good news," said Mr. Hay, joining Marshall. "You can try the ten-mile race."

When the ten-mile race was called, Marshall wheeled his bicycle over to the starting line.

"Don't try to go too fast at first," said Mr. Hay. "Just keep up with the others, if you can."

Marshall's bike shook a little as he bent down to clip his feet onto the pedals. Mr. Hay steadied it.

Marshall could feel his heart thumping hard. His hands felt slippery on the handlebars. His legs felt shaky. "One!" shouted the starter. "Two! Three!" *Bang!*

Mr. Hay pushed the bicycle so hard, Marshall could smell the dust that flew up. Marshall pushed his legs around and around.

The riders rode in a close pack. Two bicycles bumped, and one fell. Marshall rode around the fallen bicycle and rider.

Marshall pulled ahead of the pack. The boy in the red shirt passed him. Three more riders passed him, then two more.

Marshall could hear the crowd cheering. It was hard to know who was ahead, because the riders kept going around and around the track. Around and around they went. Marshall's legs hurt. "I hope I can finish the first half of the race," he said to himself.

Marshall's mouth tasted dusty. "I want to drop out," he thought. "I can't make the halfway mark."

Someone shouted, "Hooray for Marshall Taylor!" It made Marshall feel stronger. "Maybe I can finish a few more laps," he thought.

His bicycle went faster and faster around the track. His wet shirt stuck to his back, and his back hurt from being bent over. His legs hurt, too.

The people in the crowd stamped their feet and cheered. Marshall heard Mr. Hay, standing at the edge of the track, shout, "Last lap coming up next!"

Marshall pushed as hard as he could. The wheels seemed to say, "Got to finish, got to finish."

Marshall speeded over the finish line. His bicycle was going so fast he couldn't stop. He went around another lap to slow down.

Marshall heard the crowd shout something that sounded like, "Marshall Taylor! Marshall Taylor!" Hats flew into the air.

Mr. Hay hurried over to Marshall. He hugged him. "You won, Marshall. You won the race!"

"Who, me?" asked Marshall.

The judges held up their hands to quiet the crowd. Then one shouted, "Marshall Taylor is the winner!"

Marshall Taylor became the fastest bicycle rider in the world. He was called Major Taylor because he stood so straight. He was the first black American to ride in bicycle races that had both black and white racers. From 1896 to 1910, Major Taylor raced in the United States and in many other countries. He held both American and world racing titles.

Bicycle racing was an important sport in the late 1800's and early 1900's. Huge crowds went to see any race Major Taylor rode in. All the newspapers covered the story.

Major Taylor was loved by his fans for his riding skills, his fairness, and his good sportsmanship.

1. How did a bicycle race change Marshall Taylor's life?

2. What were three ways in which Marshall was uncomfortable on the long bike ride?

3. Do you think it was a good idea for Marshall to ride in a one-mile race first? Why?

4. What did the crowd do that helped Marshall?

5. When did you know that Marshall was going to win the ten-mile race?

6. Mr. Hay believed in Marshall Taylor and told him to try bicycle racing. How did this change Marshall's life?

Prewrite

Think about Marshall Taylor's surprise win in the ten-mile bicycle race. Think about how that might be reported in the news.

Copy and complete the idea burst to help you write a good headline and decide what information to include in your news story.

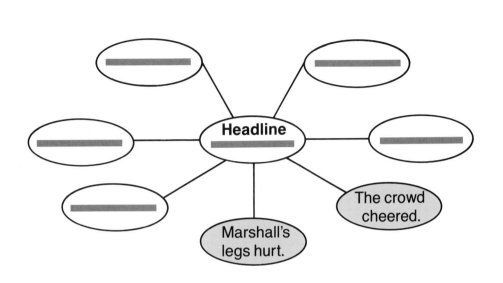

Draft

Pretend that you are a sportswriter for your local newspaper. Write a story covering the bicycle race that was described in the story.

Revise

Look over the story and then read over your paragraph. Read it aloud to yourself or a friend. Does it include all of the important information about Taylor's win? Add any details that you think would improve your story.

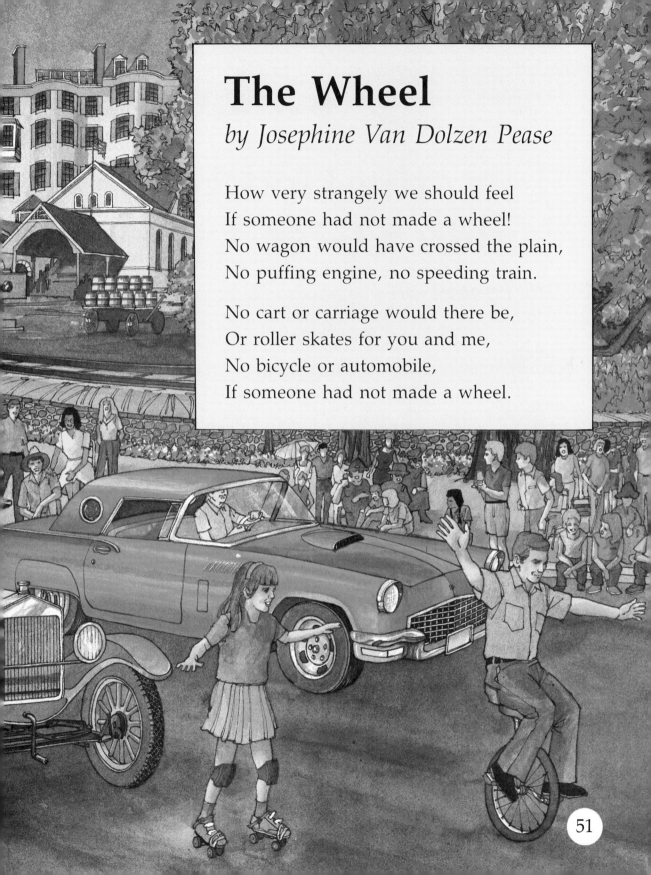

The Wheel

by Josephine Van Dolzen Pease

How very strangely we should feel
If someone had not made a wheel!
No wagon would have crossed the plain,
No puffing engine, no speeding train.

No cart or carriage would there be,
Or roller skates for you and me,
No bicycle or automobile,
If someone had not made a wheel.

51

Hilda sets out to visit her aunt. What surprises does Hilda meet along the way?

Hilda, the Hen Who Wouldn't Give Up

by Jill Tomlinson

Hilda was a hen—a small, brown hen. She lived on Biddick's Farm in a village called Little Dollop.

Hilda was very excited. Her aunt had just hatched five baby chicks. Hilda couldn't wait to see them, but her aunt lived five miles away. How was Hilda going to get there? It was much too far to walk. She sat in her favorite spot under the hedge to think. Suddenly Hilda had an idea. Of course! She would have to get a ride.

Hilda squeezed through the thick hedge and hurried down the muddy lane from the farm. Anyone could see that she was a hen who was *going* somewhere.

She went down the farm lane and along the main road toward Much Wallop. She went right through the village of Little Dollop, and past the few houses on the other side. She found nothing she could ride except a wagon in somebody's front yard. That was not much good without somebody to pull it.

Then she saw the very thing! It was big and red, shining in the sun—and the driver was just getting into it. Hilda would ride on this.

The strange thing was that other people seemed to have the same idea! Several others jumped onto it at the same time as Hilda—people with shiny helmets. Hilda had no time to wonder why. She was too busy hanging on.

The fire engine—for that is what it was—had started off with great speed. Hilda was sure she would fall off. She closed her eyes tightly as the wind blew through her feathers. The big silver bell above her head began to clang and clang.

It was all very exciting! Hilda opened her eyes and looked around her. There was a ladder just above her. She could perch more safely on that. She climbed up to the ladder and hopped right to the top. She could see for miles from up there.

Hilda was excited. They would soon be at Much Wallop at this rate. Then, to her surprise, she saw that they were turning onto a side road. This was no good—she would have to get off.

"Stop!" she squawked. "Stop! I want to get off!" Of course, nobody heard her above the noise of the bell.

Then they did stop—suddenly. Hilda was nearly thrown off her perch at the top of the ladder. The ladder began to move. Before Hilda realized what was happening, she was going up and up into the air. The ladder was being sent up to the top windows of a very tall house. Now a fire fighter could climb up and save anybody who might be trapped on the top floor.

Poor Hilda was scared. The smoking windows were getting nearer and nearer, and she did not want to be a cooked chicken!

Then the ladder came to rest against the side of the house. Hilda was glad to find that she was not to be tipped right into the fire. She heard someone coming up the ladder behind her. She was just going to look around when—whoosh!—water hit the wall beside her. Hilda was soaked.

"Oh!" shouted a voice from behind. "Watch what you're doing with the hoses down there! It's not my night for a bath!"

Then the fire fighter saw Hilda—a little bundle of wet feathers perched at the top of the ladder.

"Hello!" he said. "What are you doing up here, young lady? You don't look like much of a fire fighter to me! I'll have you down quickly. Just hang on while I look around."

He was soon back again. "There's nobody there," he said. "Come on, down we go." He gently lifted Hilda off her perch, took off his helmet, and placed her in it. Hilda had a nice ride back to earth.

It was really very kind of him, especially as she was so wet. Hilda said "thank you" in the only way she knew—she laid a nice brown egg in his helmet! He felt it there when he put in his hand to lift her out.

"Well," he said, drawing it out. "Thank you!"

The fire was out, and the fire fighters were getting back on the engine to go home. "It's Hilda—from Biddick's Farm. We'd better take her home," the fire fighter said.

So Hilda had another ride on the fire engine—but quietly this time, in the kind fire fighter's helmet. He dried her as best he could, gently put her back into his helmet, and let the sun do the rest.

When they got to Little Dollop, Hilda's fire fighter set her down at the farm gate. She clucked softly to say good-bye and then squeezed under the gate and walked into the yard. It isn't every day that a hen comes home in a fire engine!

It was only after Hilda had told the others *all* about it that she realized that she still had not seen her aunt's new chicks at Much Wallop! She would try again tomorrow.

1. What surprises did Hilda meet as she traveled to visit her aunt's new chicks?

2. What problems did Hilda have after she got on the fire engine?

3. How did the fire fighter help Hilda after she got soaked with water from the fire hose?

4. Do you think the title fits the story? Why?

5. How did the author tell you that Hilda knew that the fire fighter had helped her?

6. Hilda did not succeed in getting to see her aunt's new chicks, but she was willing to try again. How do you know this?

Think and Write

Prewrite

Think about the story "Hilda, the Hen Who Wouldn't Give Up" and decide whether or not it is a fantasy.

Draft

Choose one of the following activities.

1. If you decided that the story about Hilda *was not* a fantasy, write a paragraph proving that it was not. Use several different details from the story to convince your reader.

2. If you decided that the story about Hilda *was* a fantasy, write a paragraph proving that it was. Be sure to use details from the story to convince your reader.

Revise

Read your writing to a classmate, and then work together to add any more details that might make your writing more convincing. Even though you may disagree, you should be able to find parts of the story "Hilda, the Hen Who Wouldn't Give Up" to prove your point.

Reality and Fantasy

You have read many kinds of stories. Some are true to life and others are make believe. True to life stories are called realistic fiction. They tell about people or animals that are real, or could be real. Make-believe stories are called fantasy stories. They tell about people or animals that are not real.

Bicycle Rider is a realistic story, because it tells about Marshall Taylor, who was a real person. Realistic stories tell about characters who do things that real people could do. Realistic stories also tell about things that really happened, or could happen.

Fantasy stories can tell about people who fly or disappear, or animals who can talk or sing. Hilda the Hen was a fantasy character, because hens cannot talk in real life. Stories may also be fantasies because of what happens in them. A girl jumping high into the clouds is a fantasy. In real life, these things could not really happen, but we can pretend they happen in fantasy.

Read the following list of characters. Tell which ones are fantasy characters and why.

elves   Gina and Grandpa   Merle the squirrel

Elves and Merle the squirrel are fantasy characters because they can do things real people or animals cannot do. Elves do not exist in the real world. Squirrels exist in the real world, but they cannot talk. Gina and Grandpa are not fantasy characters. They do things that real people could do.

Now read the sentences below. Tell which ones might be in a fantasy story and which ones would be in a realistic story. Why?

1. A boy takes a bike ride over the treetops.
2. A girl finds a dog and takes it home.
3. A dog gets dressed and goes to work.

Sentence 1 might be in a fantasy because a boy could not ride a bike over the treetops in real life. Sentence 2 might be in a realistic story because a girl could find a dog and take it home in real life. Sentence 3 might be in a fantasy because a dog does not get dressed to go to work.

When you read a story, decide if it is real or make believe. Remember to look for clues in the story that help you to decide.

Kate Greenaway Medal

A dragon becomes the pet of an ordinary family. How does the dragon change their lives?

The Dragon of an Ordinary Family

by Margaret Mahy

There was a family called Belsaki—Mr. Belsaki, Mrs. Belsaki, and their little boy, Gaylord Belsaki. They were a quite ordinary family. Their house was a quite ordinary house on a quite ordinary street. They would have lived quite ordinary lives forever, if one morning Mrs. Belsaki hadn't called Mr. Belsaki a *fuddy-duddy.*

The day began with Mr. Belsaki rushing through his breakfast, a little late for work. As he was rushing out of the door, Mrs. Belsaki called after him, "On your way home, dear, stop in at the pet shop and buy Gaylord a pet."

"A pet!" cried Mr. Belsaki. "What does he want a pet for? We haven't the room, anyway."

"Of *course* he can have a pet," said Mrs. Belsaki. "We have room for an *elephant* if Gaylord wanted one."

"An *elephant*!" Mr. Belsaki turned a little pale.

"All right, all right," Mrs. Belsaki said, "he doesn't *want* an elephant. He just wants a puppy—or perhaps a little kitten. Don't be a *fuddy-duddy,* Mr. Belsaki!"

Mr. Belsaki stamped out, pulling his hat down over his ears, saying, "*Fuddy-duddy,* indeed!"

On his way home from work, Mr. Belsaki went into the pet shop and looked around. He saw white mice, cute puppies and kittens, all kinds of birds, and some sad-eyed goldfish. He also saw a parrot called Joe, with a sign over him saying "Not For Sale."

Then his eye caught a sign which said "Unusual Pet, Very Cheap." In smaller letters below, it said "Dragon, House-Trained, 50¢."

"That is a very good price," said Mr. Belsaki to the pet shop man. "I suppose it isn't a very good kind of dragon."

The pet shop man sighed. "No, it's a good kind—the *only* kind," he said. "Not very many people want dragons, you know."

Mr. Belsaki couldn't decide. The dragon winked its blue eyes at him. "I'll take it!" said Mr. Belsaki loudly.

That was how it happened that Mr. Belsaki came home with a tiny dragon in a tiny box.

"What on earth is in there?" Mrs. Belsaki asked.

"A dragon," said Mr. Belsaki.

"A dragon!" shouted Mrs. Belsaki.

"*A dragon!*" cried Gaylord.

"It's very unusual," Mr. Belsaki answered, "and it was cheap. You said I was a *fuddy-duddy,*" he added, "and I am no such thing!"

"You could have bought something pretty," Mrs. Belsaki said. "A kitten, perhaps, or a bird that talks. Where will we keep a dragon?"

"You said we have room enough here to keep an elephant," Mr. Belsaki told her. So they kept the dragon, and it grew and grew.

It was a wonderful pet for Gaylord. He kept it in the tiny box for a while, then in a bird cage, then in a dog house. He painted a washtub for its food, with the word "Dragon" on it in red.

The dragon grew and grew. Mrs. Belsaki became quite proud of it. "It certainly gives a different look to the place," she said at least once a day. "It makes us a bit unusual, too."

Her friends said, "What on earth did he get *that* for?" Mrs. Belsaki always answered, "Mr. Belsaki is a man with *ideas*, that's why!"

The dragon grew and grew. Finally it filled almost the whole yard. It got so it could breathe smoke and fire. It even got big enough for Gaylord to ride. Then it got as big as an elephant. None of Mrs. Belsaki's friends came to visit any more. They were quite afraid.

One day the Mayor came to look at the Belsakis' dragon. He studied and studied it. "It is much too big to keep in a built-up place," he said crossly. "Mr. Belsaki, you are just an ordinary family, and you should stick to ordinary pets. You must sell it to a zoo, or to a circus."

Mr. and Mrs. Belsaki looked very worried and sad. They loved their dragon, but it was getting too big. Besides, it cost so much to feed.

"We don't even have enough money to go on a vacation this year," Mr. Belsaki said sadly.

"I want to keep our dragon!" Gaylord cried.

"Well, you can't!" the Mayor answered. "You have exactly one week to get rid of it!" Then he went away.

Then the dragon turned around and faced them. For the first time, it spoke. "As a matter of fact, it *is* getting a little crowded here for me. How would you like to come for a vacation with *me* to the Isles of Magic?" the dragon asked. "*All* dragons know the way there."

Mrs. Belsaki thought a moment. "Well, it *could* be all right. I'll go and pack."

So the Mayor, Mrs. Belsaki's friends, and all their ordinary neighbors were surprised to see the Belsakis fly away on the dragon's back that very day with all their things tied to the dragon's tail.

Higher and higher the dragon flew—way up into the clouds. Then, after a long time, it dropped down, down, down. There, below them, lay a beautiful blue sea, with the Isles of Magic spread across it.

The Isles of Magic, the dragon told them as they flew along, are the homes of all the wonderful, strange, fairy-tale people. What would an ordinary family with an ordinary home do on the Isles of Magic?

They walked in the forests, the dark and old forests. They saw castles rising above the trees. They saw a princess sitting in the window of a castle combing her hair, waiting for a prince to come and save her.

They searched for gold on isles where parrots screamed in the tall trees. They saw giants that were as big as mountains.

At last the time came for them to go back home. The dragon stayed, for the Isles of Magic are the right place for dragons. As a good-bye present, the dragon gave Gaylord a tiny black kitten with an oversized purr. Then the Belsakis sailed off for home on a flying carpet.

"Now," said Mrs. Belsaki, her unpacking nearly done, "we can be ordinary people again. I was very fond of that dragon—but it will be nice to be with our neighbors again."

"Next year," Gaylord asked hopefully, "can we visit the Isles of Magic and see our dragon?"

"Who knows," said Mrs. Belsaki, a little sadly, "we may never see it again. I suppose we'll have to be just an ordinary family. Perhaps no other magic will ever happen to us again."

Just then the little black kitten woke and sat up tall in Gaylord's lap. "I wouldn't be too sure of that," it purred, and went back to sleep.

1. How did the Belsaki family become an unusual family?

2. What problems did the Belsaki family have after the dragon grew up?

3. How was the problem of getting rid of the dragon solved?

4. Do you think the Belsakis will ever be an ordinary family again? Why?

5. When did you begin to think that it might be a good idea for the dragon to stay on the Isles of Magic?

6. Having a dragon for a pet changed the Belsakis' lives. How do you know this?

Think and Write

Prewrite

Think about an imaginary pet that is so special and unusual that you might like to own.

Copy and complete the chart about your pet.

Pet: ▬▬▬▬▬▬▬▬▬▬▬▬▬	
Looks like	▬▬▬▬▬▬▬▬▬▬▬▬▬▬
What it does	▬▬▬▬▬▬▬▬▬▬▬▬▬
Why unusual	▬▬▬▬▬▬▬▬▬▬▬▬▬
How behaves	▬▬▬▬▬▬▬▬▬▬▬▬▬

Draft

Choose one of the writing activities below.

1. Write a description of your pet for someone who has not seen it.

2. Pretend that you have just bought an imaginary pet. Before you bring it home, you decide you had better write a note describing your new pet. Be sure to explain why you think your family will like it.

Revise

Read your story over again. Do the words in your story give the reader a picture of how your imaginary pet looks and what it is like? Add any new details that you think might help.

Thinking About "Voyages"

In this unit, you learned that a voyage can take you far away from home or just around the corner. Sometimes voyages do not turn out the way they are planned. How was the bicycle ride that Gina and Grandpa took different from what they had planned? Marshall Taylor's race around a bicycle track did not turn out the way he thought it would. How did this voyage change Marshall's life?

Think about some of the fantasy characters in this unit. On what voyages did the authors of these fantasies take you? Did these voyages end the way they were planned? Merle's voyage took him across the country on the tail of a kite. The Belsakis and their dragon flew away to the Isles of Magic. What adventure did Hilda have that she hadn't planned on having?

As you read other stories, look for voyages that the characters take. Are these voyages real or are they fantasies? Do the characters change because of their voyages?

1. How are the stories "Merle the High-Flying Squirrel," "Hilda the Hen Who Wouldn't Give Up," and "The Dragon of an Ordinary Family" alike? How are they different?

2. How are the stories "The Bicycle Balloon Chase" and "Bicycle Rider" alike? How are they different?

3. How was Hilda's voyage like Merle's voyage? How were their voyages different?

4. If Marshall Taylor had been in a bicycle race with Gina, who do you think would have won? Why?

5. Which of the voyages in this unit would you rather take? Why?

Unit 2
Landscapes

Landscapes are all that you see around you. Purple mountains, dry deserts, and sparkling waterfalls are part of a landscape. Fields of tall grass and blue-green oceans are part of a landscape, too. Even a small part of a beautiful garden can be a landscape.

Some people paint landscapes, while others write songs or poems about them. Do you think that different people might see the same landscape differently?

In "Landscapes," you will read about people who live on high, flat lands and on rolling hills. You will also read about an artist whose special landscape was right in his own backyard. As you read, think about why these landscapes are important to the characters. What do the characters learn from them?

Read on Your Own

A Pocketful of Cricket *by Rebecca Caudill. Holt.* Jay takes his pet cricket to school. An understanding teacher lets Jay share it with the class.

The Village of Round and Square Houses *by Ann Grifalconi. Little.* In Central Africa, there is a village where the men live in square houses and the women live in round houses. This is the tale of how that came to be.

This Year's Garden *by Cynthia Rylant. Macmillan.* A busy year in the life of a large family passes with the planting and tending of their garden.

Timothy Tall Feather *by Charlotte Pomerantz. Greenwillow.* Timothy and Grandpa tell Indian tales until they fall asleep.

Apple Pie and Onions *by Judith Caseley. Greenwillow.* Rebecca loves Grandma but is embarrassed when Grandma speaks Yiddish. Rebecca learns how to make things right again.

Juan Bobo and the Pig *by Bernice Chardiet. Walker.* Juan Bobo, a Puerto Rican folk hero, plays a trick on a pig.

Carrie Happle's Garden *by Ruth Craft and Irene Haas. Atheneum.* The children discover that a little old lady on the other side of the wall is not as scary as they had believed.

The Mare on the Hill *by Thomas Locker. Dial.* A mare learns to trust others in this gentle story. You will also see beautiful paintings that show the seasons and the new colt.

One Morning in Maine *by Robert McCloskey. Viking.* Sal spends a day on the beach with her family. She loses her loose tooth but makes a wish on a bird's feather instead.

The Skate Patrol Rides Again *by Eve Bunting. A. Whitman.* Two young detectives figure out who has been stealing pets from their apartment building.

Eleanor the circus elephant is unhappy after she is sent to live at the zoo. How does Eleanor solve her problem?

Encore for Eleanor

story and pictures by Bill Peet

Eleanor the elephant had been a great circus star for forty years. The huge elephant put on such a great act that she always left the crowd calling for more. "Encore! Encore!" everyone shouted. "Come on, Eleanor! Once more!"

Then one night, Eleanor suddenly lost her balance. Down she tumbled, to hit the floor in one huge *kerthunk!* As she lay there, everyone thought the old elephant had broken every bone. She wasn't hurt much, but the circus boss decided that Eleanor was no longer fit to stay in the show. So Eleanor was sent to live in the city zoo.

Eleanor was put into a pen with plenty of hay and water. Her elephant house was a neat red barn shaded by a big tree. "I'm lucky to be here," said Eleanor, "yet I'll never be happy unless I can perform a few tricks to earn my keep."

When people stopped at Eleanor's pen to stare at her, Eleanor felt silly just standing there. Without her fancy circus robe, she felt like an overgrown wrinkled ugly big bloop of a thing.

"If I can't look my best," Eleanor grumbled, "then I don't want to be seen at all." So Eleanor stayed out of sight as best she could.

It was a lonely life for an elephant who loved cheering crowds, bright lights, and lots of excitement. Eleanor would have gone on being lonely if someone had not come along to change things.

One day a girl came to the zoo to sketch the animals. As she set up her easel, she woke Eleanor from her afternoon nap. Eleanor had often wondered how people drew pictures. So she went across her pen to the fence, where she peeked over the girl's shoulder.

The girl was drawing the rhinoceros who lived in the pen just across the way. With a few quick strokes of her charcoal she drew the sleepy half-open eye, the stumpy horn, and the low jaw. She even put the hair on the tips of the ears! The girl's mind was made up to make her drawing as realistic as she could. So every now and then she stopped to look at the rhinoceros and decide where to put all the folds in his wrinkled skin.

Just when she was ready to draw his back legs, the rhinoceros flopped on the ground. He began rolling over and over on his back.

"Oh, no!" cried the girl. "Why couldn't that rhinoceros stay put!" She was so disappointed that she threw her charcoal onto the sidewalk. She picked up her drawing and threw it into a trash can. Then she went off to watch the ducks.

Eleanor was disappointed, too. She was about to head back to her barn, when she discovered that the charcoal was within easy reach. The sketch pad and easel were also nearby.

Suddenly Eleanor wanted very much to draw a picture. She looked to make sure that the girl was still watching the ducks. Then Eleanor took the charcoal in her trunk. Eleanor quickly drew the very first thing that came to mind—the face of Zonko the clown she remembered from the circus. To start off, she made two crisscrosses for eyes, two silly eyebrows and a long pointed nose, then a crooked grin.

Eleanor's drawing was far better than she thought it would be. She smiled to herself as she drew Zonko's big ears. Then she put a tall hat on his head. Eleanor was nearly finished when suddenly she was caught by surprise.

"I can't believe it!" cried the girl, pulling the drawing off the sketch pad. Then, waving Eleanor's clown drawing in the air, the girl shouted at the top of her voice, "Come look! Come look, everyone! Come see what this elephant drew!"

In no time at all a group of school children and their teacher ran over. They were very excited. Then the zookeeper stepped in.

"I hate to spoil your fun," he said, "but I'm afraid an elephant can't draw a picture. Even though Eleanor was once a circus performer, she is still just an animal."

"Just an animal, am I?" Eleanor grumbled. "I'll show him a thing or two!"

Once again Eleanor took the charcoal in her trunk. As everyone watched in surprise, Eleanor quickly dashed off a picture of a lion. It was old Maynard from the circus — sad eyes, whiskers, and all. She finished the sketch in only seventeen seconds!

"Great!" cried the zookeeper. "If Eleanor can draw a clown and a lion, she can draw lots of things! What do you say we put on an elephant-drawing show?"

Everyone happily agreed. Of course Eleanor was thrilled at the chance to be a star performer once more.

In less than a week, a special stage was built for the show. An extra-large easel was set up to hold extra-large sketch pads. Now Eleanor could make extra-large drawings for hundreds of children to see. Best of all, Eleanor was given a fancy new robe. Now she could look her best while she performed her act.

At the end of each show, the children always called for more. "Encore, Eleanor! Encore!" they shouted. "One more, Eleanor! Please! Draw one more!" That was sweet music to the happy old elephant's big flappy ears.

1. What were three reasons Eleanor was unhappy?

2. How did Eleanor solve her problem?

3. Who helped Eleanor solve her problem?

4. Do you think the title is a good one? Why?

5. When did you know that Eleanor wouldn't be lonely anymore?

6. How did watching the girl draw change Eleanor's life?

Prewrite

Think about how Eleanor must have felt her first night at the zoo. Think about a time when you had to leave your friends or your family. How did you feel then?

Draft

Choose one of the following activities.

When the light looked just right, he began to paint. He covered his white canvas with the colors of trees, water, and sky. When people looked at his painting later, he wanted them to see what he had seen—an early summer morning on the river.

The man in the boat lived long ago in France. He was an artist who loved the outdoors. Most of all, he loved the water. His name was Claude Monet. He is known as one of the greatest landscape painters who ever lived.

The Young Artist

Claude Monet was born in France in 1840. He spent his early years in a town where a great river ran into the sea. Claude loved the sea.

As a child, Claude was always sketching. People liked Claude's sketches. By working hard, Claude could sketch eight pictures a day and sell them.

By the time he was fifteen, Claude was already a famous artist in his home town. He sold his sketches to a shop, which hung them in the window. The shop also showed the work of another artist, named Mr. Boudin.

One day the two artists met at the shop. Mr. Boudin said to Claude, "So, young man, it's you who does these little sketches. They have something in them, but why not try painting? I will be happy to give you lessons."

At first Claude had no answer. He didn't like Mr. Boudin's paintings. He wasn't sure that he wanted him for a teacher. Finally, Claude agreed.

Mr. Boudin taught Claude how to paint sunlight and shadows. He taught Claude a great deal about painting. When the lessons ended, Claude knew that he wanted to be a painter for the rest of his life. At the age of seventeen, Claude went to the city of Paris to study more about art.

The Difficult Years

Art school was not what Claude had expected. The teachers at art school said that artists should paint in studios, not outdoors. They had many rules for what to paint and how to paint it. Claude could not follow these rules. He said, "I can paint only what I see."

Claude became very unhappy. He finally left Paris, but he held onto his ideas, and he kept on painting. Claude painted landscapes in parks, near rivers, and beside the sea.

Claude also painted large pictures, like "Women in the Garden." He painted this picture on a canvas eight feet tall. First he painted as much of the canvas as he could reach. Then he connected wires to it. He dug a hole and lowered the canvas into the hole. After he had painted the top of the canvas, he used the wires to lift the canvas out of the hole.

Each of the eight paintings shows a different part of the water garden. As you move from one painting to another, you seem to walk around the garden from beginning to end. Because of the way Monet painted these works, you see the garden from morning until night. Walking among these paintings is like spending a whole day in Claude Monet's garden.

Monet painted his *Water Lilies* until the day he died at the age of eighty-six. He was almost blind, but he kept on painting. He did not just want to paint, he needed to paint. As he put it, "I paint just as a bird sings."

1. Who was Claude Monet?

2. Why is Claude Monet still remembered?

3. What was Claude Monet's last great work, and why was it important to him?

4. Why do you think the author used subheads in this selection?

5. When did you realize that Claude Monet had his own ideas about things?

6. At first Claude Monet was not successful at selling his paintings. Why did he keep painting the outdoors?

Prewrite

Think about the ocean or a river or lake that you have seen. Think about what colors you would use if you were painting a picture. Think about how you would fill the paper or the canvas. Try to have an exact picture in mind.

Copy and complete the idea burst to help you think of details.

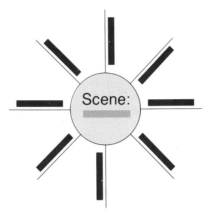

Scene:

Draft

Your job is to paint that picture with words. Write a paragraph describing the lake or river or ocean scene that you had in mind. Describe it clearly so that your reader will be able to see the same picture.

Revise

Tell one of your classmates about the picture that you had in mind. Then let him or her read your paragraph. Ask him or her if your paragraph really seems to describe the scene. Add more details to make your description really clear.

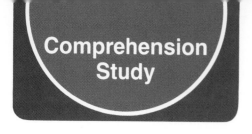
Main Idea and Details

Students in Miss Maynard's class were studying about art. They decided to work in groups. Each group would find information and report to the class. The children realized that they should plan what they wanted to learn about art. Miss Maynard showed them how to make an idea burst to organize their ideas before they began to study.

Since art was the topic, Miss Maynard wrote *art* on the chalkboard and asked the children what they wanted to learn about it. Half the children wanted to study about painting, and the other half wanted to learn about sculpture. Miss Maynard wrote *painting* on one side of the word *art*, and *sculpture* on the other side.

Then Miss Maynard asked the children what they wanted to learn about painting or sculpture. The children suggested that they study the materials used for both painting and sculpture. Read the idea burst to find out what materials the children wanted to study.

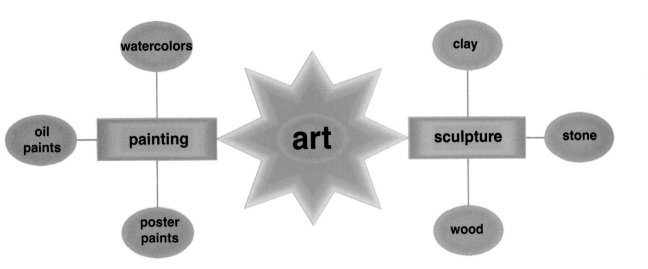

Eleanor is in the group that will study about painting. Read the paragraph that she found in an art book.

One form of art is painting. Some artists use nothing but oil paints because they like the texture of the paint on the canvas. Other artists prefer to use watercolors because watercolors to spread easily across the paper. Still other artists are fond of poster paints because of the bright colors that are available.

What is the topic of the paragraph? The topic of the paragraph is *art*. What does the paragraph tell about? It tells about painting.

That is the *main idea* of the paragraph. Which sentence gives the main idea? The first sentence in this paragraph gives the main idea. All the other sentences tell about different kinds of paint. After you finish reading, you may want to organize your ideas into an idea burst.

Textbook Application: Main Ideas and Details in Science

Read these paragraphs from a science textbook.

Rock is one of our oldest building materials. People have found many ways to use it. It is strong. Roads are made from it. So are some bridges, dams, and houses. Often, granite, marble, and limestone rock are used in buildings. Many tall office buildings in cities are made from rock.

There are many beautiful rock formations in our national parks. People come from all over the world to visit the Grand Canyon in Arizona and Yosemite National Park in California.

Gateways to Science, McGraw-Hill

What is the main idea in the first paragraph? The main idea is that rock is used in building. The first sentence is the main idea sentence. The other sentences are detail sentences. What is the main idea in the second paragraph? The main idea in the second paragraph is the beautiful rock formations. Which sentence is a detail sentence? The last sentence is a detail sentence.

Now read the information from another science book. Look for the main idea of each paragraph.

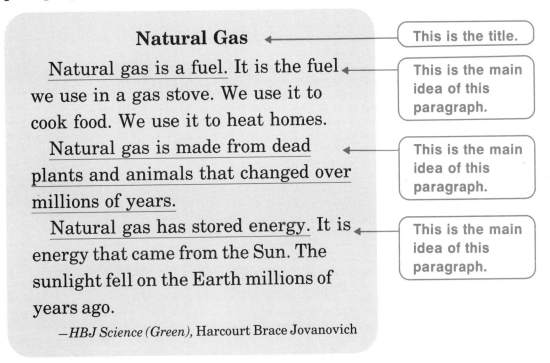

Natural Gas ← This is the title.

Natural gas is a fuel. It is the fuel we use in a gas stove. We use it to cook food. We use it to heat homes. → This is the main idea of this paragraph.

Natural gas is made from dead plants and animals that changed over millions of years. → This is the main idea of this paragraph.

Natural gas has stored energy. It is energy that came from the Sun. The sunlight fell on the Earth millions of years ago. → This is the main idea of this paragraph.

—*HBJ Science (Green)*, Harcourt Brace Jovanovich

As you read, look for the main idea in paragraphs. Read the details that tell you more about the main idea.

Children's Choices Author

Pornada

by Mary Francis Shura

After the long, cold winter, spring was almost too beautiful to believe. As if by magic, the hills of Mexico were bright with color.

Each afternoon Francisco would race home from school. This gave him more time to play in the hills with his pet pig, Pornada. Sometimes Francisco's little sister, Josi, came along.

One day, as they were going home for supper, Francisco and Pornada stopped suddenly. They saw a tall man coming down the road.

"Guido!" Francisco cried, "Guido, my friend!"
Off he ran toward Guido with Pornada racing
behind him. Josi, who was riding on Pornada's
back, held on tightly to Pornada's ears. She cried,
"Stop! Stop!" at the top of her voice.

Guido looked up the trail at them. His face
changed quickly from sadness into a smile and
then into a shout of laughter. He walked quickly
toward them and lifted Josi from Pornada's back.
He patted her hair and hugged her, still laughing.

"Welcome back, Guido," Francisco said as he
jumped with joy. "How we have missed you!"
Pornada sat up straight on his back legs. He
seemed to be welcoming Guido home, too.

"Come for supper," Francisco begged. "Mama
and Papa would be so happy to see you."

Guido said no, but the children were able to get him down the hill. Mama and Papa, watching from the doorway, welcomed him inside.

"You have traveled a long time, Guido the Gem Finder," Francisco said.

"Perhaps you should call me just *Guido* now," his friend sighed. "In all those travels I did not find the gem I was searching for. So many miles I have traveled." He sighed again.

"You found no jade?" Mama asked.

Guido shook his head. "I was so sure that for once an old legend would come true!"

"There is a legend about this jade?" Papa asked.

Guido laughed. "Such a legend. I should have laughed at it long ago. They say that where jade lies sleeping under the earth, a mist rises at dawn. They say that it is the jade itself breathing through the stone. Only artists and dreamers would believe such a tale, but I believed it. In rain and sun I have searched every dawn, and still my hands are empty."

"Francisco goes out at dawn, too," said Mama, "but he goes out to paint."

"What great sights your eyes must have seen," Papa said thoughtfully.

"Indeed they did," Guido agreed. "I have visited the caves of the Indians and walked through beautiful cities."

"But never," Francisco asked, "never once did you see the stones breathe at dawn?"

"Not once in all those months, my small friend," Guido replied sadly.

Francisco winked at Pornada. Should he tell Guido what he knew?

"Enough of my troubles," Guido said. "Tell me how you've been."

"We have been fine, mostly because of Francisco. He has worked like a man in his boy's way, helping us get through the winter," Papa said.

"No school?" Guido asked, alarmed.

"School too," Papa told him. "Along with school, he has painted and sold many of his paintings."

"Such a young artist," Guido said. "How is your painting going?"

Instead of answering, Francisco went to the shelf where he kept his new paintings. Carefully he brought one to the table. Guido looked at it. Then he leaned nearer as if to see better. His eyes opened wide and he seemed almost frightened.

"Francisco?" he asked in a frightened voice.
Francisco nodded. "What do you think?"

"This is true?" Guido asked. "This is not a
dream you had, but something you saw?"

Papa and Mama came from their places to stare
over Guido's shoulder. Even little Josi leaned
against Guido's knee for a better look.

"It is a nice painting," Papa said in a puzzled
voice. "It is a tree whose leaves have left for the
winter, a hillside, and some stones."

"And mist!" Guido cried excitedly. "Mist that
breathes from the rock! Show this place to me,
Francisco, and let us dig!"

"Pornada will lead us there," Francisco
laughed. "It is his favorite place. He would lead
me there each dawn if I would let him."

Francisco and Josi were sent to bed. The night seemed to pass slowly for Francisco. When he dreamed, his head was bright with the tales that Guido had told. In his dreams, he saw the pale mists of that rocky place.

Just before dawn, Francisco, Pornada, and Guido left. They climbed up the rocky hillside. Sleepy birds moved in the trees about them.

Then they were there. The three of them stood quietly and watched the sun come up. From the rock beneath one tree, they saw a small mist rise.

Guido started to dig. After a while, he knelt down, giving a cry of such gladness that Pornada squealed with joy, too.

"It is not very pretty," Francisco said. He and Pornada stared at the huge rock in Guido's hand.

"Wait until it has been cleaned, my friend," Guido replied.

Guido put the jade into a big brown bag and carried it over his shoulder. Dawn turned to day as they made their way down the mountain. He sang loudly as they walked down the path and into the house. Mama and Papa were getting ready for their day's work.

"My hands are not empty now," Guido roared. "Artists and dreamers—they are the real gem finders."

"I am so happy for you," Mama said, with her slow smile. "You will be as rich as you are happy."

"We will all be rich," he told her. "Half of this belongs to my friend here." He put a hand on Francisco's shoulder.

"It was Pornada," Francisco said.

"Pornada indeed. This is then the richest pig in all Mexico!"

Discuss the Selection

1. What was the old Mexican legend that Guido believed?

2. Why was Guido excited when he saw Francisco's painting?

3. How did Pornada help to prove the legend?

4. Do you think Guido was a good man? Why?

5. What told you that Francisco knew something important about the legend?

6. Guido had given up his dream of finding the jade. How did Francisco and Pornada help him make his dream come true?

Think and Write

Prewrite

A legend is a story that has been handed down from earlier times. It may or may not be true. Sometimes legends explain things that people saw in the real world. Think about something in the real world about which you could make up a legend. Share your idea with a classmate.

Draft

Write a legend using the ideas you shared with your classmate. Be sure to write as if the legend were real, and as if you really believed it.

Revise

Read your legend to yourself and then read it to a classmate. Have your partner ask two questions about your writing. Answer his or her questions. Think about the questions that your partner asked. Decide if you would like to add anything else to your legend.

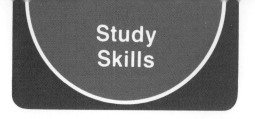

Encyclopedia

When you want to find information on a topic, one place to look is an encyclopedia. An **encyclopedia** is a set of books that contains hundreds of articles about many topics. Each book in the set is called a **volume.**

Look at the set of encyclopedia shown below. Notice that each volume has a letter or letters on it. The books in the set are arranged in alphabetical order.

A	B	C-Ch	Ci-Cz	D	E	H	I	J-K	L	M	N-O	P	Q-R	S-Sn	So-Sz	T	U-V	W-X Y-Z
1	2	3	4	5	6	9	10	11	12	13	14	15	16	17	18	19	20	21

Finding Information in an Encyclopedia

The topics within each volume are also arranged in alphabetical order. The volume marked "A" contains articles on any topic that begins with the letter *a*. In the "A" volume, you could find information about Africa, the Alamo, or ants.

Topics having more than one word are alphabetized by the first word. For example, if you wanted to find information about New York, you would look in the "N" volume. Where would you look to find information about the Rocky Mountains? Yes, you would look in the "R" volume.

If you want to find information about a person, use the first letter of the person's last name. You would find an article about Claude Monet in the "M" volume of the encyclopedia under "Monet." Where would you find an article about Benjamin Franklin? Yes, you would find it in the "F" volume under "Franklin."

Suppose you want to find out where sequoia trees grow. You would first look in the "S" volume under "sequoia" because that is the name of the special tree that interests you. If you can't find the information there, look in the "T" volume under "tree."

Suppose you wanted to find out about African and Indian elephants. Would you look up "Africa," "India," or "elephants"? Since the topic is elephants, you would go to the "E" volume.

Using the Encyclopedia

Look at the picture of the encyclopedia on page 108. Tell the letter of the volume you would use to find information on each of these topics:

1. Alexander Calder
2. legends
3. New Mexico
4. jade
5. South America
6. pearls
7. Betsy Ross
8. George Washington
9. corn oil
10. pine trees

Suppose you have been asked to report to your class about a gem and you have picked jade as your topic. You already know how to spell and say the word. You know from the story "Pornada" that jade is a gem. To find out where jade is found, what it looks like, how it is used, and other interesting facts about jade, you could use the encyclopedia.

In the "J" volume of the encyclopedia, you find that there are other topics that begin with the letters *ja*. How would you find *jade*? Yes, to find *jade*, you have to go to the third letter of the word *jade*, the letter *d*. Now you can begin reading about jade.

Young Reader's Choice Author

Encyclopedia Brown is known as a good detective. How does he solve this case?

The Case of the Cave Drawings

adapted from the story by Donald J. Sobol

Elmer Evans came into the Brown Detective Agency.

"You look worried," Encyclopedia told him. "Is something wrong?"

"Plenty," answered Elmer. "It's that Wilford Wiggins."

Wilford Wiggins was a high school boy with lots of get-rich-quick ideas.

"What's Wilford up to now?" Encyclopedia asked.

"Down to," corrected Elmer. "He climbed down that hole into the old bear cave the other day."

"Good grief!" exclaimed Encyclopedia. "All kids are supposed to stay away from that bear cave. The hole could be dangerous."

"Wilford has called a secret meeting for five o'clock at the cave," said Elmer. "He's going to tell all the kids what he found in the hole. He says he'll make us all rich."

"Wilford didn't ask me to the meeting," said Encyclopedia.

"I bet he's still mad at you," said Elmer. "He'll never forget how you spoiled his sale of Hercules Strength Tonic last month."

"That stuff was nothing but colored water!" exclaimed Encyclopedia. "I think I'll go to the meeting with you."

The bear cave was a mile outside the town line. When Encyclopedia and Elmer got to the bear cave, a crowd of boys and girls had already gathered outside the cave to hear Wilford.

Wilford raised his hands and called for quiet.

"Do you kids know what's inside this cave?" he asked.

"Sure we know," said Bugs Meany. "There's a lot of rock and a hole in the floor that goes down to China."

Wilford laughed.

"You want to know what I found at the bottom of that hole?" cried Wilford. "Another cave, even bigger than the one on top. On the walls were drawings—done by cave people!"

A thrill of excitement ran through the children.

"We'll keep this a secret, okay?" said Wilford. "If some smart grown-ups hear what's down in that hole, they'll buy this land in a hurry. They'll make a lot of money by charging people three dollars a ticket to see those cave drawings!"

The children nodded. There was a fortune in it!

"I can rent this land," said Wilford, "but I need a little more money. Then I can dig an opening to give people a better way to get into the lower cave."

"I knew you'd ask us for money," said Rocky Graham. He was a member of the Tigers, a club for tough older boys.

"Get lost, kid," said Wilford. To all the others he said, "I'm going to let each and every one of you buy a piece of this business for five dollars. We'll all make a fortune."

"How do we know that those walls have cave drawings on them?" asked Benny Breslin.

"After I found those cave drawings, I went home and got my camera," said Wilford. "I took pictures with a flash."

He passed out three photographs. The first was of a wooly rhinoceros. The second was of cave people attacking a dinosaur. The third was of a charging mammoth.

"There's the proof!" shouted Wilford. "For five dollars you'll all get a share of every ticket sold. So go home and get your money, but don't breathe a word of this to anyone!"

"Maybe I spoke too quickly, Wilford," Rocky Graham said. "I'm sorry. I've got ten dollars saved. Can I buy two shares?"

"Sure, sure, kid," said Wilford. "I don't have the heart to keep anybody from a really big money-making deal like this."

Rocky and the other Tigers raced for their bikes. They talked about using the club's money to buy all the shares themselves.

Encyclopedia watched the Tigers pedal away. Then he told the rest of the children to hold onto their money.

"No cave person drew those pictures," he said.

How did Encyclopedia know? Turn the next page upside down to find out.

Solution to "The Case of the Cave Drawings"

Encyclopedia knew that Wilford Wiggins had drawn the cave pictures himself and then had photographed them.

One of the photographs that Wilford passed out showed a drawing of "cave people attacking a dinosaur." That was Wilford's mistake! Since it is unlikely that the cave artists even knew about dinosaurs, they could not have known what a dinosaur looked like.

Because of Encyclopedia's sharp eye, Wilford went out of the cave business!

119

1. How did Encyclopedia Brown become interested in the case?

2. What clue helped Encyclopedia Brown solve the case?

3. What clue helped Encyclopedia Brown stop the children from giving Wilford their money?

4. Do you think Wilford was a nice person? Why?

5. How does the author let you know that the Tigers thought only about themselves?

6. What do you think Wilford learned from Encyclopedia Brown?

Prewrite

Wilford's story was almost believable because long ago people really did make drawings in caves to tell stories. Think about some symbols or pictures that you could use to tell a story. What kind would you use? For example, these pictures could stand for a person, mountains, a river, and a tree:

Draft

Write a story using only pictures or a combination of words and pictures. Try to use more pictures than words.

Revise

After you finish, think about how your story reads. Does it tell the reader what you want it to? Is it easier to use words or pictures only?

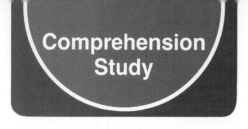

Compare and Contrast

How are the two pictures alike? Both are dinosaurs. How are they different? One dinosaur is larger than the other. One is brown, and one is green.

When we think about how things are alike, we compare them. When we think about how things are different, we contrast them.

Read the three pairs of sentences below. Each group of sentences tells about Francisco and Wilford. Which group helps you know the most about Francisco and Wilford?

1. Francisco likes to ride in a boat. Wilford also likes to ride in a boat.
2. Francisco likes to ride in a sailboat. Wilford likes to ride in a canoe.
3. Both Francisco and Wilford like to ride in boats. Francisco rides in a sailboat, and Wilford rides in a canoe.

The last group of sentences compares and contrasts the children. This group of sentences helps you know Francisco and Wilford better.

Read the paragraph below. See how two animals are compared and contrasted.

Elephants and squirrels are animals that live in Africa. Elephants grow to be very big. They live on the ground. Squirrels are small and live in trees. Elephants eat plants and seeds. Squirrels eat plants and seeds also.

How are the animals alike? How are they different? The chart helps you compare and contrast.

Compare (alike)
Elephants live in Africa. Squirrels live in Africa. Elephants eat plants and seeds. Squirrels eat plants and seeds.
Contrast (different)
Elephants are big. Squirrels are small. Elephants live on the ground. Squirrels live in trees.

As you read, be sure to look for comparisons and contrasts. These comparisons and contrasts will give you clearer pictures of the characters and their setting.

Children's Choices Author

Johnny has a problem. How does his sister Kate help him solve his problem?

The Cave

by Eleanor Clymer

This story is taken from a chapter of *The Spider, the Cave and the Pottery Bowl.* Kate and her younger brother Johnny spend each summer with their grandmother, who lives on a mesa.

Each year, Kate helps Grandmother make pottery, but this year there is no more clay. While Kate is holding a bowl which had belonged to the Old Ones — their Indian ancestors — Johnny bumps her arm. The bowl falls to the floor and smashes. Johnny feels very bad about this and goes to search for another bowl. As this story begins, Kate is going to look for Johnny.

"Grandmother," I said, "did you see Johnny this morning?" Grandmother said she hadn't seen him. I thought that since Johnny had broken the old bowl, he might have run away. Then I said to Grandmother, "I will see if I can find him."

She nodded and said, "He is troubled about the bowl. Tell him it does not matter. I am not angry."

I wrapped some food in a cloth. I put it in a basket and took a bottle of water. Then I started out.

It was lovely on the mesa early in the morning. The air was cool and fresh. When the sun came up, it made the houses look as if they were painted with light red paint.

From where I stood, I could see far out over the desert. The mesa stretched out for miles. Many kinds of desert plants grew on it.

I started to walk away from the village. I saw where twigs and leaves had been broken. I thought that must be the way Johnny had gone.

The valleys in the mesa were like big cracks in a table top. Some of those valleys were wide and had good soil for planting corn. We called them washes, because when there was a thunderstorm, the water washed down them like a flood. People put little fences around the plants so they wouldn't be washed away.

I looked up at the sky and thought, "I'm glad
it's not going to rain today"—though we had
been hoping for rain because it was so dry. But
there were only white clouds in the blue sky, the
fluffy kind that never do anything.

I was coming to one of those washes. The path
led down the slope to cornfields at the bottom. I
was getting very hot. The sun beat down on my
head, and I wished that I had a hat. I took a drink
of water. I was glad I had it.

Then I was ready to start down into the valley.
It wasn't steep like the edge of the mesa, but it
was pretty far down. I thought, "How do I know
Johnny is down there?" I squinted my eyes. Yes,
down in the valley I saw a boy on a burro. They
looked very tiny. I yelled, "Johnny!" But of
course he couldn't hear. So I started down.

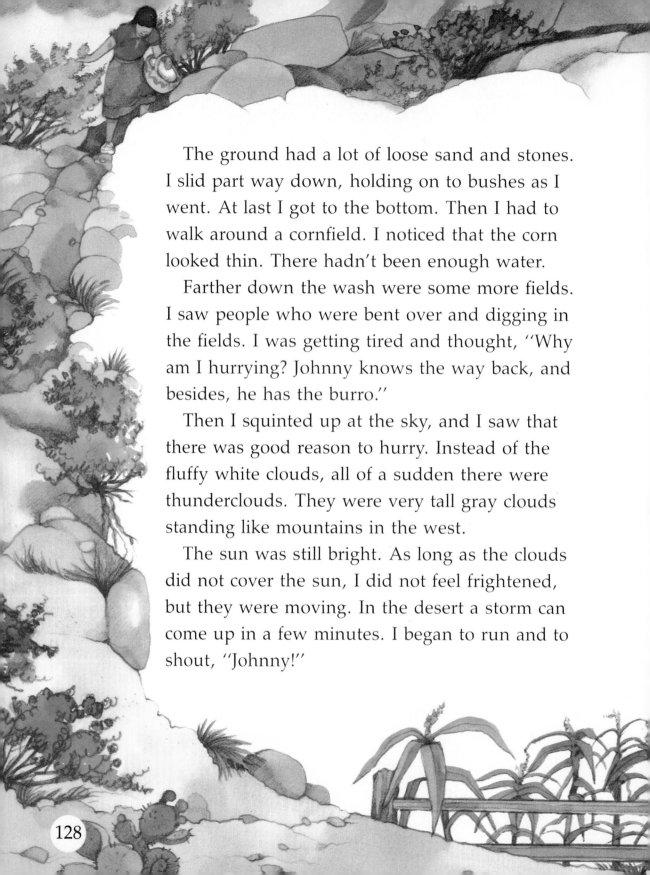

The ground had a lot of loose sand and stones. I slid part way down, holding on to bushes as I went. At last I got to the bottom. Then I had to walk around a cornfield. I noticed that the corn looked thin. There hadn't been enough water.

Farther down the wash were some more fields. I saw people who were bent over and digging in the fields. I was getting tired and thought, "Why am I hurrying? Johnny knows the way back, and besides, he has the burro."

Then I squinted up at the sky, and I saw that there was good reason to hurry. Instead of the fluffy white clouds, all of a sudden there were thunderclouds. They were very tall gray clouds standing like mountains in the west.

The sun was still bright. As long as the clouds did not cover the sun, I did not feel frightened, but they were moving. In the desert a storm can come up in a few minutes. I began to run and to shout, "Johnny!"

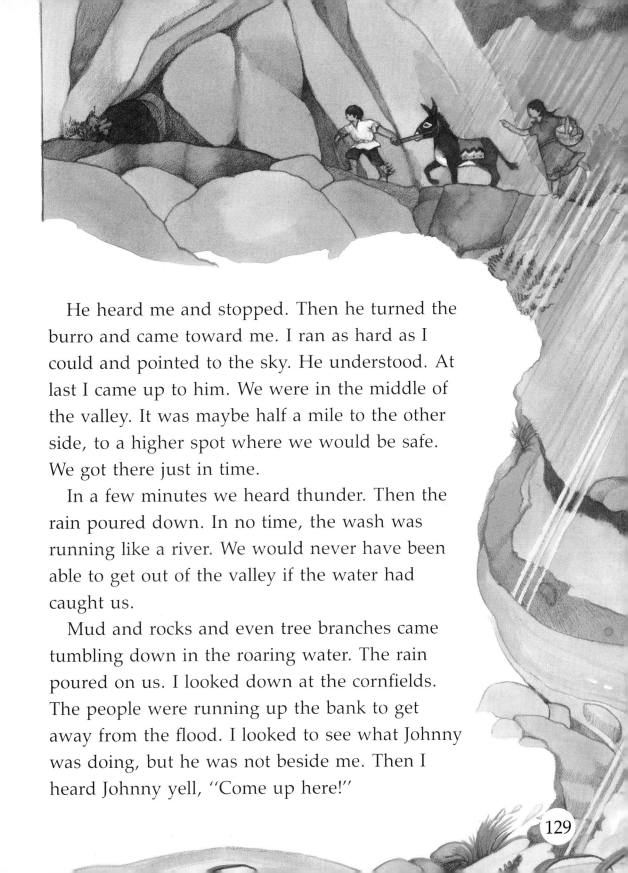

He heard me and stopped. Then he turned the
burro and came toward me. I ran as hard as I
could and pointed to the sky. He understood. At
last I came up to him. We were in the middle of
the valley. It was maybe half a mile to the other
side, to a higher spot where we would be safe.
We got there just in time.

In a few minutes we heard thunder. Then the
rain poured down. In no time, the wash was
running like a river. We would never have been
able to get out of the valley if the water had
caught us.

Mud and rocks and even tree branches came
tumbling down in the roaring water. The rain
poured on us. I looked down at the cornfields.
The people were running up the bank to get
away from the flood. I looked to see what Johnny
was doing, but he was not beside me. Then I
heard Johnny yell, "Come up here!"

He had found a cave, really an overhanging arch in the rock. Johnny was standing there out of the rain. I pulled the burro and went up there, too. We sat down and watched the rain fall. We sat for a long time. Finally I asked, "Where were you going?"

He said, "I was sorry I broke Grandmother's bowl. I wanted to find another one in the place where our ancestors lived. I didn't know how far it would be, so I took the burro."

I said, "Where were you going to look? I don't see any ruins around here."

We stood up and looked at the rock shelter we were in. At the back, under one end of the arch, there was a crack. It was really a hole in the rock, partly filled with stones and sand. We noticed that a thin stream of water ran out of it.

"Let's go in," Johnny said. "It looks like a deep hole. Maybe there are some ruins inside."

I shouted to Johnny, "Don't go in!" It was too late, however. He was inside the hole. I felt frightened, but I could not let him go in there alone. I tied the burro to a bush and crawled in after Johnny.

It was pretty dark inside. When my eyes got used to the darkness, I saw Johnny at the back of the cave.

"Did you find anything?" I asked.

"Yes," said Johnny. "An old basket, and a stick."

I went over to the basket. I dragged it closer to the light and looked inside.

Johnny said, "It's just a lot of dirt. I wanted to find pottery."

I said, "Johnny, you did!"

He thought I was joking. He said, "It's only sand."

I said, "It's not sand. It's clay! There's clay in this cave. Look! It's the same kind of clay that Grandmother uses to make pottery! You didn't find an old bowl, you found something better! Now we will be able to make our own bowls again with Grandmother."

1. What was Johnny's problem?

2. Why was the old basket that Johnny found in the cave important?

3. How did Kate help Johnny?

4. Would you like to have Kate for a sister or friend? Why?

5. How did you know that Grandmother was not upset about the broken bowl?

6. Kate and Johnny found a cave to keep them dry when the storm came. What other problem did finding the cave help them to solve?

Think and Write

Prewrite

Think about a time when you broke something of value or did something to make your parents or grandparents sad. How did you feel?

Problem: ▬▬▬▬▬▬▬▬	
What happened	▬▬▬▬▬▬▬
When it happened	▬▬▬▬▬▬▬
Where it happened	▬▬▬▬▬▬▬
Why it was important	▬▬▬▬▬▬▬
How I felt	▬▬▬▬▬▬▬
How I solved it	▬▬▬▬▬▬▬

Draft

Write a story that explains what you did that you felt bad about. Be sure to include what happened, why it was important, and how you felt about it. Also, explain what you did, like Johnny, to try to solve the problem.

Revise

As you revise your story, be sure that it includes what caused a problem, why it was important to you and your family, and what your feelings were about what happened. Have you also included how you tried to solve the problem?

Corn-Grinding Song
A poem of the Zuñi Indians

Lovely! See the cloud, the cloud appear!
Lovely! See the rain, the rain draw near!
    Who spoke?
Twas the little corn-ear
High on the tip of the stalk
Saying while it looked at me
    Talking aloft there—
"Ah, perchance the floods
    Hither moving—
Ah, may the floods come this way!"

135

*Plants and animals can be found in a desert.
How are they able to survive?*

The Desert:
What Lives There

by Andrew Bronin

The desert is a place that gets very little rainfall. The ground is often sandy and rocky. When the sun beats down, the sand and rocks grow hot and dry. It is hard to imagine that a place like this is full of living things.

All living things need food, shelter, and some kind of protection to survive. Some plants and animals make their homes in the desert because they have found these things there.

How Do Living Things Get Water?

A cactus plant is at home in the desert. The cactus has a special way of getting water in the dry desert soil. It spreads its roots out close to the top of the ground. When rain comes, the cactus roots soak up all the water they can.

Once a cactus plant gets water, it saves the water for the dry days ahead. A cactus stores up enough water in a rainstorm to last a long time.

The desert tortoise is also at home in the desert. It gets most of the water it needs from the plants it eats, but it drinks water, too. When it rains, the tortoise drinks all the water it can. It stores the extra water under its shell. It can live for months without another drink.

The kangaroo rat is another animal at home in the dry desert. It can make water inside itself from the dry seeds that it eats. It never has to take a drink of water in its life.

How Are Living Things Protected?

The cactus, the tortoise, and the kangaroo rat can live in the desert because they know how to get water. However, water is not the only thing that plants and animals need to survive in the desert. They also need protection.

The kangaroo rat can protect itself. When a snake or a fox tries to catch it, the kangaroo rat jumps high into the air, like a kangaroo. It can also kick sand into its enemy's face. All the snake or fox gets is a mouthful of sand!

The tortoise can also protect itself. It just pulls its legs and head into its tough shell. Not even the strongest animal can bite through a tortoise shell.

The cactus protects itself, too. It has sharp spines all over its stem. Animals would eat the juicy cactus if it didn't have spines. Because the spines are so sharp, most animals won't touch the cactus.

Some plants and animals are at home in the desert because they get along well with each other. The gila woodpecker is very much at home with the cactus. Its enemies would love to eat the gila woodpecker, but it has found a way to keep safe. The gila woodpecker uses the cactus' spines for protection. It pecks a hole high in the tallest cactus. There it builds a nest. Its enemies can't climb the cactus to get it.

The elf owl doesn't know how to peck a hole in the cactus, but it does the next best thing. It waits until a gila woodpecker leaves its nest. Then it moves in. The elf owl needs the gila woodpecker, just as the gila woodpecker needs the cactus.

Where Do Living Things Hide?

The sun makes the desert sand very hot. Many desert animals don't like the heat, but there are no caves to hide in and no trees to curl up under. These desert animals spend their days underground, away from the hot sun.

The pack rat lives underground. It digs a hole and fills it with odds and ends that it finds in the desert. In a pack rat's hole you might find anything from a feather to a piece of an old car.

Badgers live underground, too. They dig holes and spend the day there. Badgers come out at night when it's cooler to hunt for food.

Some animals can't dig their own holes. They have learned to let other animals dig for them. The desert cottontail is like the elf owl. Since the desert cottontail can't dig its own holes, it moves into holes that other animals have left.

Could You Survive in the Desert?

If you were alone on the desert, do you think you could survive? You could, if you learned from the plants and animals that live there.

You know that you could get water from the cactus. You could also take shelter underground. For you, however, the desert would always be a strange place. For the plants and animals that get along well together in the desert, the desert is not a strange place at all. It is home.

1. How are some plants and animals able to survive in the desert?

2. How do some desert plants and animals get along well together?

3. How do the cactus, desert tortoise, and kangaroo rat protect themselves?

4. What is the most interesting fact you learned from this article?

5. How do you know that the author thinks people would not like living in the desert?

6. What things do both plants and animals need to survive in the desert?

Think and Write

Prewrite

Think about how life is *different* in a desert from where you live.

Copy and complete the chart that follows.

Unit 3

Applause

Have you ever clapped your hands after a funny play or when a home run is hit in a baseball game? Applause is a way of telling people that you are pleased with what they did. People like to hear applause. It tells them that others understand them and like them.

Applause is just one way of telling people that you are pleased with what they did. Telling people in words is another way. Sometimes the look on your face is enough to show how you feel. What are some other ways to share your feelings or to praise others?

In "Applause," you will meet people who express themselves in different ways. As you read these stories, think about how the characters share their good feelings with one another.

Read on Your Own

Clara's Dancing Feet *by Jean and Joanna Carey Richardson. Putnam.* Clara is upset when she does not perform well at her first dancing class.

Oma and Bobo *by Amy Schwartz. Bradbury.* Oma is not happy to have a dog but will teach it to behave in the house.

Come Back, Amelia Bedelia *by Peggy Parish. Harper.* Amelia Bedelia can not do anything in the expected manner.

White Dynamite and Curly Kidd *by Bill Martin, Jr., and John Archambault. Holt.* Little Kidd watches her dad, Curly Kidd, ride the rodeo and dreams of doing the same thing.

Sam *by Ann Herbert Scott. McGraw.* No one in the family seems to have time for Sam.

Georgia Music *by Helen V. Griffith. Greenwillow.* A little girl shows her love for her grandfather.

My mother and father went to a school for deaf children when they were growing up. That's where they learned to talk. They learned by placing their fingers on their teacher's throat and feeling how words felt in her voice box as she said them. They learned how words looked by watching her face, especially her lips, as she spoke. It's hard to learn to say words that way, but my parents did learn to talk.

They don't talk much now, but they can talk. Since they have never heard other people talking or even their own voices, they don't know how voices sound. It's not always easy to tell what they are saying, but Gina, Diane, and I can understand them.

When we communicate with our parents, most of the time we talk with our hands as well as with our mouths. One way to communicate with your hands is to learn a special alphabet so you can spell words with your fingers. This is called finger spelling.

Another way to communicate with your hands is to use sign language. Learning to sign is like learning a whole new language. You have to learn the same signs that other people have learned so that you can be understood. Most of the time one sign stands for one word, but sometimes it can stand for more than one word. Once you have learned sign language, it is much faster to use than finger spelling.

Gina, Diane, and I are learning new signs all the time. Mother and Father learned sign language when they were little. They taught us signs when we were babies, just as hearing parents teach their children words. Our grandparents, friends, and neighbors helped us learn to talk.

Sometimes my mother and father understand what people are saying by reading their lips. That's another thing my parents learned at their school—lipreading.

Reading lips is hard. Some people don't move their lips much when they talk. Some people hide their mouths with their hands. Besides, many words look alike when you say them. Look in the mirror and say "pin" and "bin," "hill" and "ill." See what I mean?

The way we move our bodies and the way our faces look when we talk help our parents read our lips. Most of the time we talk to them with our hands. Our grandmother says we have words in our hands.

My parents have some interesting things to help them. In our house, when the telephone or doorbell rings, lights flash on and off. We also have a special machine attached to our phone. It types the messages onto paper. Then my parents can type messages back.

Of course, the people calling us must have the same kind of machine attached to their telephones, and not very many people do. That means that many times we have to talk on the telephone for our parents.

Some deaf people have a hearing ear dog to help them. Our dog, Polly, isn't a trained hearing ear dog, but she can do many things a hearing ear dog does.

Polly can get my parents up by tugging at their covers if the flashing-light alarm doesn't wake them. If the doorbell rings, Polly will run back and forth to let my mom and dad know someone is at the door.

We are a happy family. At least we were until about six months ago. Then the company where my father has always worked moved to a new town, one hundred miles away.

It took a long time to get used to our new town. In our old town, nobody stared when they saw us talking with our hands. In the new town, people did stare. They pretended they didn't see us, but I knew they were looking.

One day Gina's favorite teacher gave her a note to take home asking for our family to go to a play by the National Theater of the Deaf. Gina said that the play would be in sign language. Who would understand it better than our parents?

The night of the play, the big hall was filled with people. Just inside the door, my mother signed to me, "Where will we sit?"

To our surprise, a man stood up and signed, "There are five seats over here."

We couldn't believe it. He was talking to us in sign language! All around us, the people in the audience were talking with their hands.

We learned from the program that some of the actors were deaf and some could hear. During the play, the hearing actors and some of the deaf actors would speak. All of the actors would sign, sometimes for themselves and sometimes for each other. Everyone in the audience would be able to understand what was going on in the play.

I was proud of my parents. They were smiling, and their fingers were flying as fast as anyone's. For the first time in months, they seemed to feel at home.

Then we had another surprise. Gina's teacher came over to us. She talked very slowly and very carefully so my parents could read her lips. Then she signed with her hands!

Gina was excited. Her favorite teacher, who wasn't deaf, had words in her hands, too. We were learning there were many friendly people in our new town who could talk with our parents. This place wasn't going to be so bad, after all.

After the play, we went backstage to meet the people in the acting company. The deaf actors talked with people who knew sign language. The hearing actors helped the other people understand what was being said.

I think some of the hearing people around us were learning something, too. Being deaf doesn't mean a person can't hear or talk. If they have to, people can hear with their eyes and talk with their hands.

1. What does "words in our hands" mean?

2. What are three ways in which Michael communicates with his parents?

3. How did Gina's favorite teacher help the Turner family?

4. Do you think the Turner family is happier in their new home now? Why?

5. When did you first know the Turners went from a happy family to an unhappy family?

6. Michael and his family went to a play at the National Theater of the Deaf. Why was this important?

Think and Write

Prewrite

Think about what it would be like to have a friend who was deaf. Pretend that you are going to play with two friends. One is deaf and one is not. Use the following chart to help you explain what it would be like to play with your friends.

What Like	Problems

Draft

Write directions for the hearing friend so that she or he will know what to do to communicate with your friend who is deaf.

Revise

Check over your directions to see if they are clear and specific. Be sure to check to see if you have included all the steps. Make any changes that you think will improve your work.

Shh
by Eve Merriam

National Council of Teacher's of English
for Excellence in Poetry

If I covered up my ears
I couldn't hear
car horns honk
garbage cans clang
screen doors bang
toasters tick
or crickets crick

or telephones ring
or foghorns hoot
or grease spatter
or fire crackle
and sigh to ash

or paper crumble
or thunder crash
or the squeak of a rocker
or the shout of a crowd
or the crack of a nut
or a motorboat's putt.

But
could I hear a feather
or a snowflake
or a cloud?

This is an interview with an actor from a theater of the deaf. How do these actors communicate?

Listen With Your Eyes

by Janice Cooper

The circus is coming to town! Soon you will hear loud happy music, and lions roaring, and people laughing. You will hear the booming voice of the ringmaster telling about each act.

But what if you couldn't hear these sounds? What if you couldn't hear at all?

In the following interview, actors from a theater of the deaf in Cleveland, Ohio, tell about their special circus of signs. Come along with the Fairmount Theater of the Deaf as they present the "Smircus"!

Question: What is the Smircus?

Answer: The Smircus is one of the plays performed by the Fairmount Theater of the Deaf. The play used to be called "Circus of Signs." It was thought up by two of our actors, Adrian Blue and Debbie Taylor. Adrian, who is deaf, had the idea for a circus that was performed using different kinds of communication. We use mostly sign language and pantomime in the Smircus. Very few words are spoken in our show.

Question: Then how do hearing people understand what is happening in the Smircus?

Answer: Hearing people may be able to understand some of the signs because they look like what they mean. But everyone can understand pantomime.

Question: Are pantomime and sign language alike?

Answer: Yes, but they have one big difference. Pantomime is a special form of art, while sign language is for everyday communication.

Question: Do you have real circus acts in the Smircus?

Answer: Yes! We have a juggler, a tightrope walker, and a snake charmer. We even have trained bears that roller-skate!

Question: It sounds as if the Smircus is quite a show! Do you perform it in many different places?

Answer: We perform in schools and in theaters. We have also performed on television. Our first television show was about "Beauty and the Beast." We have taken the Smircus with us to perform in several different countries, too. In one of the countries we visited, Smircus won an award as the show that the audience liked best.

Question: What else does the Fairmount Theater of the Deaf do?

Answer: This year we are giving a lot of school workshops. We teach children a little about acting. We help them learn pantomime, too.

Question: Do you work only with deaf children?

Answer: No, but since we are a deaf theater, we
especially try to help children who have hearing
problems. One of our dreams is to make videotapes
to help teach deaf children. We want deaf
children to understand that being deaf is not a
bad thing. It's important that deaf children know
that they can do everything that hearing people
can do, except hear. We try to show deaf people
that there are ways to communicate without
spoken words. Using sign language puts words
in their hands. Deaf people learn how to listen
with their eyes.

1. How do the actors in a theater of the deaf communicate?

2. What do the actors want deaf children to understand?

3. What does "listen with your eyes" mean?

4. Would you like to go to the Smircus? Why?

5. How do you know that people like the Smircus?

6. What are some ways you know to communicate without words?

Think and Write

Prewrite

Think about what it would be like to communicate a story with no words. Think of a story that you would like to tell in pantomime.

Draft

On paper, write a plan for a pantomime story. An example would be to tell about riding a bicycle or building a house. Be sure to include all of the different things you will need to do. Try to keep it simple, but make sure your plans are very precise.

Revise

Look over your plans and think about acting them out. Use your plan as your script and practice acting out your pantomime with a partner. If your partner doesn't understand why you are moving in a particular way, change your action to make it better.

Context Clues

When you are reading, you may come to a word that you do not know. Sometimes the **context,** the other words in the sentence, will give you clues to the meaning of the word.

Read the following sentence. Look for clues in the sentence that will help you understand the meaning of the word *theater.*

Gina and Diane went to the *theater* to see a new play.

What words in this sentence help you know the meaning of the word *theater*? The words *went to* give you a clue that a theater is a place. The words *see a new play* help you know what kind of a place a theater is. The context of this sentence helps you know that a theater is a place to see a play.

Read the sentence on the top of the next page. Look for context clues to help you figure out the meaning of *pantomime.*

The lady told the story in *pantomime,* in which she acted but said no words.

In this sentence, *in which she acted but said no words* tell you what form of storytelling pantomine is.

Now read the following two sentences. Which sentence has context that helps you know the meaning of the word *videotape*?

1. Josh and Steve watched a *videotape* of the baseball game.
2. A *videotape* is a special kind of tape on which images and sounds are recorded to be played back at another time.

Sentence 2 tells you the meaning of the word *videotape*. However, the context in sentence 1 helps you know that a *videotape* is something people can watch. Both sentences have context that help you understand the meaning of *videotape*.

When you come to a word whose meaning you do not know, look at the other words around it. Context may give you a clue to the meaning of the unknown word, as in sentence 1. Some context may tell you exactly what the word means, as in sentence 2.

Textbook Application:
Context Clues in Social Studies

Read the following paragraphs from two social studies books. The sidenotes will show you how context clues help you understand the meaning of new words.

Communication is an important word. Look at the context for help. The next sentence tells you exactly what *communication* means.

The context of this paragraph tells you two ways that people communicate.

You use telephones, phonographs, radios, tape recorders, and television without thinking them strange. They are part of everyday life.

All of these things are forms of **communication.** Communication is the way people trade thoughts and information.

The first way people communicated was by talking. And it was the only way, for a very long time. Then about five thousand years ago, people found a way of writing things down. For the first time, words didn't float away as soon as they were spoken. A message marked in wet clay could be kept or even carried from one place to another.

—*City, Town, and Country*, Scott Foresman

Changes in Communication

People have always needed to communicate and share ideas. Long ago people had only a few ways to communicate. They could talk with each other or write letters. There were no radios, televisions, or telephones until people **invented** them. *Invent* means "to make something that no one else has ever made."

Some people have always searched for new and better ways to share information. Their inventions have changed the ways in which we communicate today.

—*Communities and Resources*, Silver Burdett

Invented is an important word. What does it mean?

As you read, you can probably figure out what new words mean by using context clues.

Actors in a play like to hear applause at the end of a performance. Who gets the applause in this story? Why?

Hattie the Backstage Bat

story and pictures by Don Freeman

The backstage of a dark, empty theater is a lonely place. Only a bat would feel at home there. To a little bat named Hattie, this *was* home.

She had lived in the theater all her life. She had never seen a tree or a haunted house. Hattie's sky was the open space high above the stage.

Every night Hattie flew about for hours. She flew in and out of the ropes and between the stage curtains. When she was tired, Hattie landed in her favorite place and went to sleep.

The only person who knew about Hattie was Mr. Collins. He came to the theater every morning to sweep the floor and keep things neat.

There hadn't been a show in the old theater for quite a long time, but Mr. Collins was never lonely. He had Hattie to keep him company. Once he made Hattie a tiny hat out of odds and ends he found in an old trunk.

Each day at noon Mr. Collins shared his lunch with Hattie. Since Mr. Collins knew that bats like to eat flowers, he always brought Hattie a daisy.

While they ate, Hattie listened to Mr. Collins. He talked about the plays that had been on that stage.

One afternoon Mr. Collins had important news to tell Hattie. "Starting today, some actors will be coming here to rehearse for a new play," he said. "You'll have to stay out of sight. People get very frightened if they see a bat flying around."

Day after day, the actors came in and rehearsed their parts. Since this was a mystery play, the actors spoke their lines mostly in whispers. Soon they knew all their lines by heart. Day after day Hattie kept well out of sight. It was only late at night that she flew down to the stage to eat the delicious treats Mr. Collins had left for her.

One morning Hattie woke up to the sound of hammering. The scenery for the play was being set up on the stage. There below, Hattie saw not only a tree, but a three-story house that looked like it was haunted! The scenery was built to order for a bat!

Weeks went by. Finally there was the dress rehearsal. Hattie watched in surprise. An actor was wearing a long black cape. He looked like a huge bat! Then he began to climb in and out of the windows of the house.

"Why doesn't he fly the way I do?" Hattie said to herself. "I could show that actor how to act like a bat." Still, Hattie didn't move.

At last, it was the opening night. Everybody backstage was nervous and excited. Mr. Collins was the most nervous of all. Would Hattie stay out of sight on the most important night of all?

In the theater, the audience was beginning to settle into their seats. Since they had come to see a mystery play, they were ready to be frightened.

The lights went out and everyone was quiet. Slowly the curtain went up. The actor dressed as a bat entered. He tiptoed across the stage.

The audience groaned. They had seen plays about bat-people many times before. "I wanted to see a scary play," said one lady, sighing.

"So did I," whispered another. "How boring!"

There was one small bat in the theater who was not bored. "It's a great night for a bat like me!" thought Hattie. She could hold herself back no longer!

Spreading her wings wide, Hattie flew down through the open attic window. As she flew across the spotlight, she made a huge shadow that spread across the whole stage!

The men and women screamed! The audience became wild with fear when it saw that a real bat was flying above their heads. The screaming was just too much for Hattie. All at once, in plain sight, she flew back through the attic window.

The audience stood and cheered. "Bravo, bat!" they shouted. "Bravo!" Hattie had indeed saved the show.

So, of course, Hattie was asked to perform her wonderful flying act every night after that. She was a great star. Each night after the show, Mr. Collins proudly presented a delicious white rose to Hattie.

1. Who got the applause at the end of this story? Why?

2. Why did Mr. Collins give Hattie a white rose after each show?

3. How did Hattie save the show?

4. Do you think Mr. Collins was a nice man? Why?

5. When did you know that Hattie was not going to be able to stay out of sight?

6. Hattie took the risk of being seen. How did this change her life?

Think and Write

Prewrite

Hattie became very famous for her work in the theater. Think about what it would be like to be a famous bat. Think about some questions that you might like to ask Hattie.

Draft

Pretend that you are interviewing Hattie about what it was like to live in a theater and work in a play. Write a list of questions that you want to ask. Then write what you think Hattie's answer would be to each one.

Revise

Look over your questions and answers. Do they let a reader learn more about Hattie? Are the questions good, and do Hattie's answers really answer the questions? Revise any questions or answers that need improving.

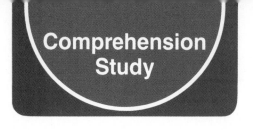
Reader Awareness

Gina read a paragraph from a book. Read to see what Gina thinks about the paragraph.

The men and women began to scream. The audience became wild with fear. One man said, "Doing that should be against the rules. I will talk to someone about it."

Gina thought that the paragraph did not make sense. She decided to read it again. Read what she found as she reread.

A bat flew across the stage and into the theater. The men and women began to scream. The audience became wild with fear. One man said, "Doing that should be against the rules. I will speak to someone about it."

Why does this paragraph make more sense? You can better understand what the man was going to talk to someone about. He was speaking about the bat that flew into the theater.

Gina decided that she was not thinking as she first read. She had to reread to get the meaning.

Now read this paragraph from a story.

Michael was proud of his father's new *rig*. It was big and shiny. People turned to look at it. Michael wanted everyone to see them.

Does this paragraph make sense to you? It may if you know the word *rig*. Pretend that you don't know the word. Now read the next paragraph from the same story.

Michael liked riding beside his father as they drove along the road. He was much higher than all of the cars. Only a few other trucks were as high.

Notice that reading on helped you get a better understanding of the word *rig*. Sometimes reading ahead helps you make sense of something you might not understand. Sometimes you need to reread to understand what you've just read.

How does Sammy find a way to be in the next family picture?

All Except Sammy

by Gladys Yessayan Cretan

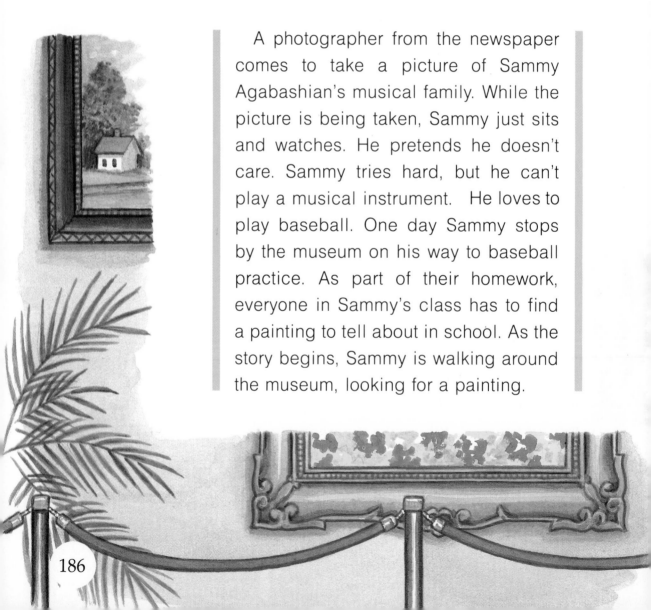

A photographer from the newspaper comes to take a picture of Sammy Agabashian's musical family. While the picture is being taken, Sammy just sits and watches. He pretends he doesn't care. Sammy tries hard, but he can't play a musical instrument. He loves to play baseball. One day Sammy stops by the museum on his way to baseball practice. As part of their homework, everyone in Sammy's class has to find a painting to tell about in school. As the story begins, Sammy is walking around the museum, looking for a painting.

"There!" Sammy said. "There's a picture I could talk about." He stopped and looked for a long time at a painting of a soldier sitting tall on a proud black horse.

Across the quietness, a voice said, "Hi, Sammy!" Sammy turned to see his friend Jason standing in front of a large picture of the sea.

"Hi!" said Sammy. "Did you find your picture?"

"I guess I like this one," said Jason. "It looks like a big storm. What about you?"

"I'll tell about this one," Sammy said. "We had better go now. We're going to be late for the game, and they can't start it without us."

The next day Sammy told his class about the picture of the soldier and the horse he had seen at the museum. "That horse could run like the wind," Sammy said.

Jason looked puzzled. "How could you tell?"

"You could see it in the picture!" said Sammy. "I could tell that from the way the muscles were drawn, and from the proud way the horse held its head. We'll stop there after school on the way to the ball park. I'll show you."

Later, as they stood in front of the picture, Sammy said, "Look at the power in that horse. Look at those muscles. You mean to tell me that horse can't run?"

After a long look, Jason shook his head. "That's a lot to tell from a painting," he said.

Sammy nodded. "It's a lot for someone to show, with just a little paint. I'd like to learn how to do that."

As they left the museum, Sammy pointed to a sign near the door. It said there was a painting class for children on Saturday mornings.

"Look!" Sammy said. "That's for me."

They walked down the wide steps and then turned toward the ball field. Suddenly Jason thought of something.

"Hey!" he said. "Sammy! What about Saturday baseball practice?"

"I'll only be a little late," Sammy said. "I wouldn't miss practice."

"What about Tug Smith?" said Jason.

"We decided in the tryouts," said Sammy. "I play first base, and he's my substitute."

Across the field they could see Tug standing at first base like he owned it. Sammy and Jason walked up to him. "Hi," said Tug. "I'm playing first base today, since you're late."

189

"Listen," said Sammy. "I'm going to be late on Saturdays, too, because I have to take a class. You're my substitute, fair enough, but I was picked to play first base. I'll be here as fast as I can."

"There's no school on Saturday," said Tug.

"I know," said Sammy. "This is a special art class at the museum."

"Art?" laughed Tug.

"Listen," Sammy said. "Can you paint a horse that looks like it can really run? Can you use gray, orange, and white, and still make a cape that looks red?"

Tug shook his head. "I can't either," said Sammy, "but that's what I'm going to try to learn. So I'll be late on Saturdays. You can be my substitute till I get here."

So every Saturday, while Sammy's mama gave music lessons downstairs, his brother and sister practiced their instruments upstairs. His papa went to band practice. Sammy went to art class.

"What about the baseball team?" Papa asked as he walked one morning with Sammy toward the museum. "I get there a little late," Sammy said. "The fellows don't mind because I'm painting a poster to show when we're playing."

"They're lucky to have an artist on the team," said Papa. "Look at the trouble we have getting our program covers planned. Our posters for the front of the concert hall don't even look like musical posters. They look like circus posters! Well, here's the museum. Learn well!"

191

When Jason got to the museum to pick Sammy up, Sammy was sitting quietly in front of a picture of a little girl. "Studying something new?" asked Jason.

"Blue," said Sammy. "This week I'm studying blue. Look," he pointed, "look at that blue dress. It's part green and part black, but it all looks blue."

"That's a fact," said Jason. "I never saw it that way before." He picked up Sammy's mitt and gave it a punch. "We get to use the big field today," he said. "Can you play late?"

"Sure," said Sammy. "There's no use going home early today, anyway. There's a photographer coming to take a picture of the family."

"You're in the family," said Jason.

"I know," said Sammy, "but he only wants the musicians in the family—everyone but me."

"Never mind, Sammy," said Jason. "Maybe you can't play an instrument, but you sure can draw."

"That's true," said Sammy. "I can draw. I've been thinking. Why can't I make the program poster for their concert? I'll bet I could plan a good poster."

Sammy worked very hard for days and days. Sometimes he painted at the museum, and sometimes at home. One day Sammy's brother called, "Look! Look at Sammy's poster!"

His sister said, "This is better than any poster we've ever had." It was, too.

So the next time a photographer came, he put Sammy right in the middle of the family, holding his poster. When the picture of all the Agabashians was in the newspaper, they were called "an artistic family."

"Boy!" said Sammy. "Look at that! I finally got in the picture."

"Why not?" said his father. "Must everyone play an instrument? No. You are an artist—and a good one!"

"Not only that," said his brother, "he's a good ball player. The big game is tomorrow, too."

"We'll be there," said Papa, "all of us."

"Sounds like music to me!" Sammy said.

1. How did Sammy find a way to be in the next family picture?

2. Why is "All Except Sammy" a good title for this story?

3. Why did the photographer call the Agabashians "an artistic family"?

4. Do you think Jason was a good friend? Why?

5. What clues in the story support Sammy's statement, "That horse could run like the wind"?

6. All of the other people in Sammy's family were musical. How were Sammy's talents different?

Prewrite

Sammy sometimes felt left out of his family until he learned to paint and until his family learned to appreciate his different talents. Think about a special skill or a talent that you have. Is it something you can do very well?

Think about how you would describe your special skill to someone.

Draft

1. Write about your special skill. Start out by telling your reader what your special skill is. Then describe it and explain how you feel about your talent. Describe a time when your talent was important to you.

2. Write about a time when someone in your family or someone important to you noticed and appreciated your special talent. Explain how it was important and how you felt when others gave you credit for your talent.

Revise

Let a classmate read your story back to you and then listen to his or her story. Ask each other questions. Discuss the lead, or first sentence and the ways you could make it better. Now, make any necessary changes in your story to make it clearer.

Biography and Autobiography

A **biography** is the true story of a person's life. It is written either about the whole life or part of the life of that person. The author of a biography is someone other than the person whose story is being told. The true story of the life of Claude Monet written by someone other than Monet is a biography.

A special kind of biography is called an **autobiography.** When a person writes the true story of his or her own life, the story is called an autobiography. You are the only person who can write your autobiography.

Read the titles and authors of the following books. Which ones are autobiographies?

1. *Anne Frank: The Diary of a Young Girl* by Anne Frank
2. *Annie Oakley and the World of Her Time* by Clifford L. Alderman

3. *Journey into Childhood: The Autobiography of Lois Lenski* by Lois Lenski

4. *Homesick: My Own Story* by Jean Fritz

If you said that *The Diary of a Young Girl, Journey into Childhood,* and *Homesick* are all autobiographies, you are right. *Annie Oakley and the World of Her Time,* however, is not an autobiography because it is the story of Annie Oakley's life told by another person.

Think about the kind of information you might find in a biography and an autobiography. Tell which information from the following list you might find.

1. The time and place the person was born

2. Make-believe stories

3. Who the person's parents were

4. Important events in the person's life

If you said that you might find the time and place the person was born and important events in the person's life, you are right. You might also find out who his or her parents were. You would not find make-believe stories because biographies and autobiographies tell real facts about real people.

The difference between a biography and an autobiography is the person who wrote it.

Tomie dePaola is an award-winning artist and author. What does he write about? Where does he get his ideas?

Meet Tomie dePaola

by Cynthia S. Ciando

The only way to get to Tomie dePaola's house is to go down a winding country road, past a lake and many maple trees. Tomie lives in a farmhouse called Whitebird, tucked into a small New England village.

What was once a barn is now dePaola's studio. On one wall of his studio hangs a pink banner with paper cutouts of some of his characters. Some children in Minnesota gave him this banner. The children shaped the *o* in *Tomie* like a heart because dePaola often uses hearts in his pictures.

Tomie dePaola started to work on children's books by drawing the illustrations for them. He says, "As an artist, it is fairly easy to decide which stories I will do." He sometimes draws the illustrations for other authors' books, but he also writes and illustrates his own books. He says, "Writing my own stories presents a whole different set of problems. The first is that I still find writing difficult. I try not to get set ideas about pictures until after I have written the story. Once the story line is good and strong, then I can let my pictures not only illustrate the story, but add to it."

Some of dePaola's books tell about things that happened when he was little. He mixes the facts with fiction and turns these ideas into stories. He also makes some of his characters seem like his friends or people in his family. The characters in two of his books, *Nana Upstairs and Nana Downstairs* and *Now One Foot, Now the Other,* are very much like his grandparents.

He says that the idea for *The Knight and the Dragon* came from a poster he did for the American Library Association. He remembers that the poster had been hanging on his studio wall for months, when suddenly the idea for the book hit him. "I wish that all ideas were *that* simple," he says. "Children often ask me where I get my ideas. I tell them that I get ideas everywhere. Of course, not every idea is a good one. The boring ones usually go quietly away."

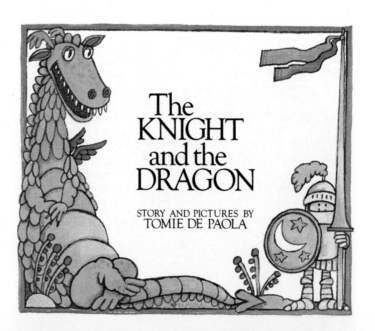

Tomie dePaola has an interesting way of making sure that he doesn't run out of ideas for new books. Before he finishes one book, he usually gets ideas for his next one. "Then I have time to get the old brain and heart going. The important thing is the heart," dePaola says. "It *must* be the best work I can do at the moment."

Tomie dePaola loves children. He says, "I don't think of children as being children. When I find myself in the company of children, I never realize that we're different ages. They're just shorter!" Then that special laugh of his spills out.

When dePaola visited Portland, Oregon, he helped to open a playground. Over 400 children watched as he cut the ribbons holding balloons. Inside the balloons were the children's names, addresses, and telephone numbers. The children hoped they would hear from the people who found the balloons. As the balloons were drifting out of sight, one child whispered, "I hope my balloon lands at Tomie's house."

Tomie dePaola talks with hundreds of children when he is on a trip. He likes to know what they are thinking. He feels it is important for children to meet the authors of the books they like to read. He thinks that "it makes the books come alive for them."

"Books have always been important to me," dePaola says. "My dream is that through writing and drawing pictures, people I've never met will get to know me a little better. I dream that I can somehow touch their lives."

Making a dream like this come true is not always easy—even for a man like Tomie dePaola. "Making a book is one of the hardest things in my life," he says. "Still, I wouldn't have it any other way. Books are my life. Meanwhile, I'll keep working, doing the best I can, and who knows? Maybe that dream will come true."

1. What are two ways Tomie dePaola gets ideas for his stories?

2. Who is Tomie dePaola?

3. Why does Tomie dePaola write books?

4. Do you think Tomie dePaola will continue writing stories for children? Why?

5. How do you know Tomie dePaola writes his stories before he illustrates them?

6. Writers often get ideas for stories from events that have happened to them, or they write about the people they know. What are some ideas you could use when writing stories?

Prewrite

The story tells us that Tomie dePaola sometimes writes stories about things that happened when he was little. Think about when you were little.

Now look at the idea burst that follows. How might you finish these thoughts?

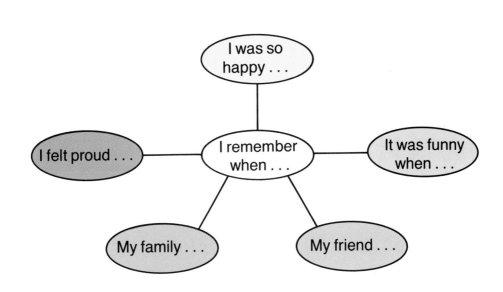

Draft

Write a story about something that happened to you when you were little. Like dePaola, you may mix facts with fiction. Try to keep the story simple and direct.

Revise

Remember what dePaola says: "The important thing is the heart. It must be the best work I can do at the moment." Read your story again and think, "Does my writing tell the story the very best I can tell it?"

Caldecott Honor Book Illustrator

In this story, how does Bob help Bobby?
How does Bobby help Bob?

Now One Foot, Now the Other

story and pictures by Tomie dePaola

Bobby was named after his best friend, his grandfather Bob. When Bobby was just a baby, his grandfather told everyone, "Bobby will be three years old before he can say Grandpa, so I'm going to have him call me Bob."

"Bob" was the first word Bobby said. Bob was the one who helped Bobby learn to walk.

"Hold on to my hands, Bobby," said his grandfather. "Now one foot, now the other."

206

When Bobby was older, one of the best things he and Bob did was to play with some old wooden blocks. The blocks had letters on two sides, numbers on two sides, and pictures of animals on the last two sides.

Bob and Bobby would slowly, very slowly, put the blocks one on top of the other, building a tall tower. Sometimes the tower would fall down when only half the blocks were piled up. Sometimes the tower would be almost finished and Bob would say, "Just one more block."

"That's the elephant block," Bobby would say.

They would carefully put the elephant block on the top. Bob would sneeze and the tower would fall down. Bobby would laugh and laugh.

"Elephants always make you sneeze, Bob," Bobby would say.

Then Bob would sit Bobby on his knee and tell him stories. "Bob, tell me the story about how you taught me to walk," Bobby would say.

His grandfather would tell Bobby how he held Bobby's hands and said, "Now one foot, now the other—and before you knew it . . ."

Not long after Bobby's eighth birthday, his grandfather got very sick. Bobby came home from school and his grandfather wasn't there.

"Bob is in the hospital," Dad told Bobby. "He's had what is called a *stroke*."

"I want to go see him," Bobby said.

"You can't, honey," Mom told him. "Right now Bob's too sick to see anyone. He can't move his arms and legs, and he can't talk. We'll just have to wait and hope Bob gets better."

Bobby didn't know what to do. He didn't
want to eat; he had a hard time going to sleep
at night. Bob just had to get better.

Months and months and months went by and
Bob was still in the hospital. Bobby missed his
grandfather.

One day when Bobby came home from
school, his father told him that Bob was soon
coming home.

"Now, Bobby," Dad said, "Bob is still very
sick. He can't move or talk. When he sees your
mother and me, he still doesn't recognize us,
and the doctor doesn't think he'll get better.
Don't be frightened if he doesn't remember you."

Bobby *was* frightened. His grandfather didn't
remember him. He just lay in bed. When Dad
carried him to the living room, Bob sat in a
chair. He didn't talk or even move.

One day, Bob tried to say something to
Bobby, but the sound that came out was awful.
Bobby ran out of the room.

"Bob sounded like a monster!" Bobby cried.

"He can't help it, Bobby," Mom said.

So, Bobby went back to the room where Bob
was sitting. It looked like a tear was coming
down Bob's face.

"I didn't mean to run away, Bob, I was
scared. I'm sorry," Bobby said. "Do you know
who I am?"

Bobby thought he saw Bob blink his eye.

"Mom, Mom," Bobby called. "Bob knows
who I am."

"Oh, Bobby," Mom said. "You're just going
to upset yourself. Your grandfather doesn't
recognize any of us."

Bobby knew better. He ran into the small
sewing room, under the front stairs. He took
the blocks off the shelf and ran back to where
Bob was sitting.

Bob's mouth made a small smile.

Bobby began to build the tower. Halfway . . .
almost to the top . . . only one block left.

"Okay, Bob," said Bobby. "Now the elephant
block." Bob made a strange noise that sounded
like a sneeze. The blocks fell down and Bob
smiled and moved his fingers up and down.

Bobby laughed and laughed. Now he knew that Bob would get better.

Bob did get better. Slowly, he began to talk a little. It sounded strange, but he could say "Bobby" just as clear as day. Bob began to move his fingers and then his hands.

When the weather got nice and warm, Dad carried Bob out to a chair set up on the lawn. Bobby sat with him.

"Bobby," Bob said, "story." So, Bobby told Bob some stories.

Then, Bob stood up very slowly.

"You. Me. Walk," said Bob.

Bobby knew exactly what Bob wanted to do. Bobby stood in front of Bob and let Bob lean on his shoulders. "Okay, Bob. Now one foot." Bob moved one foot. "Now the other foot." Bob moved the other.

By the end of the summer, Bob and Bobby could walk to the end of the lawn. Bob could talk better and better each day.

On Bobby's next birthday, Bobby got out the blocks again. Slowly he built up the tower— only one block to go.

"Here, elephant block," Bob said.

Bobby put it on top. Then Bob sneezed!

"Elephants always make you sneeze, Bob," Bobby said. "Now, tell me some stories."

Bob did.

Then Bob said, "Bobby, tell story how you teach Bob to walk."

"Well, Bob, you leaned on my shoulders and then I said, 'Now one foot, now the other,'— and before you knew it . . ."

1. How does Bob help Bobby? How does Bobby help Bob?

2. What does the title "Now One Foot, Now the Other" mean?

3. How did Bobby know that Bob was getting better?

4. How would you have felt if Bob was your grandfather?

5. How did you know that Bob was unhappy when Bobby ran out of the room?

6. Bob and Bobby were friends. How can friends help each other?

Prewrite

Bobby and Bob were best friends. Think about some of the words you might use to describe your best friends. Without using a name, tell a classmate about someone who is very special to you. Use the following chart to help you share things about your friend.

Windows

Windows are more than just panes of glass. You can look into a window and see what is happening inside a room. You can look out of a window and see what is happening outside. A window can even be anything that helps you to see or learn something new.

Did you ever think that something like your grandmother's old quilt could be a window to the past? How can museums, legends, or folktales help us look into the past? What kind of lesson do you think you could learn from a garden or a treasure chest?

As you read the stories in this unit, you will look through many different kinds of windows. Look beyond the words and pictures on each page. Think about the windows used by each character to help him or her look at life differently.

Bean Boy *by George Shannon. Greenwillow.* Bean Boy is alone in the world with only his cup of beans.

Bea and Mr. Jones *by Amy Schwartz. Bradbury.* Bea and her Dad change places. They are very successful and funny too.

A Story, A Story *by Gail Haley. Macmillan.* This African folktale tells how the spider man became the story keeper.

The Wobbly Tooth *by Nancy Evans Cooney. Putnam.* Elizabeth Ann's wobbly tooth will not come out. Find out how she solves her problem.

Handtalk Birthday: A Number and Story Book in Sign Language *by Remy Charlip, et al. Macmillan.* Friends celebrate a birthday with a deaf girl, using words, pictures, and sign language.

The Other Emily *by Gibbs Davis. Houghton.* Emily is upset to find there is someone else with her name.

What Kind of Family Is This? *by Barbara Seuling.*
Western. Jeff moves in with his new stepfather
and his son and daughters when Jeff's mother
remarries. Jeff is not happy with his new
family.

Mrs. Gaddy and The Fast-Growing Vine *by*
Wilson Gage. Greenwillow. Mrs. Gaddy buys a
goat to get rid of a vine that is taking over her
house. When the vine is gone, she must think
of a way to get rid of the goat.

Ben and the Porcupine *by Carol Carrick. Houghton.*
Christopher is afraid his dog Ben will be
seriously hurt by the porcupine in the woods.
He cannot lock up Ben, so he must figure out
a way to outwit the porcupine.

The Spider *by Margaret Lane. Dial.* This book
describes different kinds of spiders and their
habits. It also tells why spiders are important.

Who are the members of the just plain Rosedale Quilting Club? Why was this club formed?

Sam Johnson and the Blue Ribbon Quilt

by Lisa Campbell Ernst

One morning when his wife Sarah was out of town, Sam Johnson found that the awning over the front porch was torn. That night, Sam sat down to mend the tear. He took cloth from Sarah's scrap bag to mend the hole.

222

At first it was hard work. As the evening passed, Sam began to have fun picking different scraps of cloth. It was morning before he leaned back to look at his night's work.

"How beautiful!" he said. "Just wait until Sarah sees this awning! She'll be mighty proud."

Mrs. Johnson returned later that afternoon. Sam was waiting for her on the porch. "That's very nice, dear," she said, giving the awning a quick look.

"Don't you think it's beautiful, Sarah?" Sam asked. Mrs. Johnson did not answer. Sam went on, "I had *so* much fun doing it, I've decided to join your quilting club!"

"Now, Sam, dear," Mrs. Johnson chuckled. "It's very nice that you enjoyed yourself while I was away, but join my quilting club? Don't be silly."

The next night, Sarah and Sam rode together to the weekly meeting of the Rosedale Women's Quilting Club. When they walked through the door, all the women turned and stared.

Sam cleared his throat. "Good evening," he said. "I've decided to join your club."

After a few seconds, a small chuckle was
heard. Then there was another, and another.
Soon everyone in the room was laughing—
everyone, that is, but Sam.

"Don't be silly," the club president said. "Our
most important quilt of the year is coming up.
It's the one for the county fair contest. Why
don't you go join the men's Checkers Club if
you want something to do with your time?"

Sam walked out of the room. The next day he
hung posters all around the county, asking the
men to meet at his barn.

That evening, Sam spoke to all the men of Rosedale. He told them what had happened, and about the quilt contest at the county fair.

"Are you ready," Sam asked, "to show that we can do more with our hands than plow a field?" "Yes," answered a small group of voices.

"Then we should make a quilt for that contest ourselves!" Everyone clapped and cheered. The Rosedale Men's Quilting Club had just begun. Sam was made president of the club.

The county fair was only a month away. The men met every night in Sam's barn to work on their "Flying Geese" design. The women were also hard at work on their "Sailboats" design. In the week before the fair, each club worked far into the night.

On the day of the contest, each club folded its quilt. Then each quilt was put in the back of a wagon and taken to the fairground. It was a cool, clear morning after a night of heavy rain.

As the two wagons passed through the gates
of the fairground, the members of the Rosedale
quilting clubs nodded their heads to each other
in greeting. Suddenly a huge gust of wind blew
up. Both quilts were swept into the air. Each
landed in a giant mud puddle!

Neither group could believe what had just
happened. "All that work," Sam Johnson groaned.
"All those hours and hours. Now look! Ruined!"

Then the women looked at the men's quilt
and noticed how beautiful it was. The men saw
for the first time that the women's quilt was
quite beautiful, too. "You really did a wonderful
job," they said to each other. "It's too bad that
neither of our groups will win."

"I have an idea!" Sam cried.

All that morning and all that afternoon, the
Rosedale Men's Quilting Club and the Rosedale
Women's Quilting Club worked together. They
carefully cut out the clean parts of each quilt.
Then they pieced them together. As the sun set,
the last stitches were being made.

Then the judging for the fair began. Elijah
Pool's hog won a blue ribbon for being the
heaviest hog. Harriet Eyman's apple bread won
every baking prize.

As for the quilting contest, the blue ribbon
was awarded to the just plain Rosedale
Quilting Club.

"What's the name of your unusual design?"
Sam Johnson was asked.

He thought for a moment. Then he replied,
"Why, 'Flying Sailboats,' of course!"

1. Who are the members of the "just plain Rosedale Quilting Club"?

2. Why was the club formed?

3. Why was the name "Flying Sailboats" chosen for the quilt?

4. How do you think Sam felt after he went to the Women's Quilting Club meeting? Why?

5. When did you realize that once Sam made up his mind, he would not give up?

6. The Rosedale Women's Quilting Club and the Rosedale Men's Quilting Club cooperated. How did they solve the problem the men and women had at the fair?

Prewrite

Sam Johnson and the Women's Quilting Club learned a good lesson in cooperation. Think about a time when you have cooperated with a friend, or when two groups have cooperated, and then accomplished something together. Share that experience with a classmate.

Draft

Now that you have shared your story with a classmate, write a story together about cooperation. This type of writing is called collaboration. Use the examples that you shared earlier in your story. Remember that you are co-authors and that usually when two people work together, good results can be accomplished.

Revise

Look together at what you have written, and read the story to each other. Check your lead sentence and your ending to make sure that they help the story stay together. Make any changes that you think might improve your story.

How is a quilt made? What kinds of quilts do people make?

The Great American Quilt

by Carole Ann Baker

Long ago, it was unusual for old clothes to be thrown away. The parents' old clothes were made smaller to fit their children. Any extra pieces of cloth went into the scrap bag. When the bag was full, it was time to make a patchwork quilt.

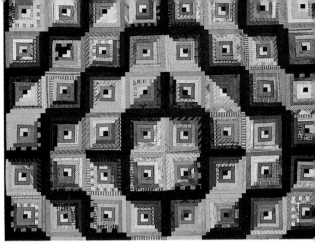

At first, these scraps did not look much like a quilt. They were just pieces of cloth in many colors and sizes. Making all of these scraps look as if they belonged together was one of the jobs of the patchwork quilt maker. The other job was then to stitch the quilt together, using a fancy design.

People who made quilts were like artists without brushes or paint. Tiny bits of cloth and fancy stitches became beautiful designs. The ideas for these quilt designs came from everyday life. One pattern called "Log Cabin" came from the way the logs in a cabin wall looked. Another one, called "Sunshine and Shadow," looked like plowed fields.

Children were taught to quilt as soon as they could hold a needle. Older children sometimes made a quilt to welcome a new baby into a family. These quilts were passed down from family to family.

Making a Quilt

A quilt is made the same way a sandwich is made. Cloth is used for the top and bottom layers, just like bread. Long ago, old cotton, wool, straw, cornhusks, and even old letters were used as stuffing for the quilt.

It took a long time to make a patchwork quilt. Usually, only the top of the quilt was made from the scraps of cloth. Sometimes scraps of cloth were used for both the top and the bottom layers. When it was time for the quilt to be stuffed and stitched together, a quilting bee was often held.

Early in the morning, whole families met in the largest home or town building. The quilters started by stretching the bottom layer of the quilt onto a wooden frame. The quilters sat around the frame to work on the quilt. They sewed three of the edges of the top and bottom layers together. Next the quilt was stuffed. Then the three layers were sewn together with tiny stitches. These stitches were made close together in a design. When all the stitches were done, the last edge was sewn together. Then the quilt was finished.

The quilters worked quickly. They stopped only to eat. Even small children were given an important job. They had to keep the needles threaded for the quilters. That helped the quilters work faster. If more than one person brought a quilt top to the quilting bee, several quilts could be finished in one day.

Friendship Quilts

One kind of quilt is a friendship quilt. Long ago, a friendship quilt was made and given to a person or family who was moving away. It was a sign of friendship from the people who had made the quilt.

The top of a friendship quilt was put together from blocks of cloth. They were all the same size. A group of people would plan the quilt design. Then each person would make a block for the quilt. People's names were sewn onto the quilt block they had made.

Sometimes a saying was sewn on a quilt block. One of the favorite sayings was "When this you see, remember me." Sometimes birds, flowers, or animals made from cloth were stitched onto the quilt block, too. Later all the people would meet to sew the blocks together.

Quilting Today

Many people in America like to save quilts and other things from the past. These old things made by hand help us remember the people who made them. Because quilting is an art form that helps us know about the past, some old quilts are kept in museums.

Today people are still making quilts. They are not just copying old patterns but also are designing new ones. People will probably make quilts for years to come. All that is needed to make a quilt is bits of cloth, needles, thread, and imagination.

1. What is needed to make a quilt?

2. What quilt patterns were described in this selection?

3. Why do some people like to save quilts?

4. Would you rather make or receive a friendship quilt? Why?

5. How did the author help you to "see" the layers of a quilt?

6. Quilting is an art form that tells us about the past. How does a quilt tell us about the past?

Prewrite

Think about something you can make or do. Look back at the story to see how making a quilt is explained in an interesting way.

Copy and complete the chart that follows, and write the steps that you might use to explain to someone about how to make or do something.

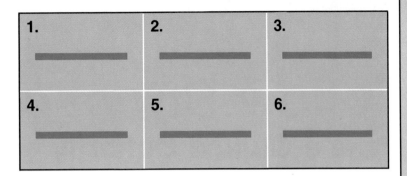

Draft

Write a story explaining exactly how to do something. Be sure to put in order the things that must be done. As you write, be sure to make each step in the process clear for your reader.

Revise

Read your story to a classmate. Ask each other questions. These questions may give you some help in knowing where you need to add more information. Look over your story again and add anything that might make it clearer.

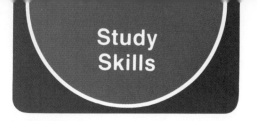
Follow Directions

Make a Quilted Butterfly

Sam Johnson and the men in Rosedale enjoyed making a quilt for the county fair. People have enjoyed making quilts for hundreds of years. By following directions, you will learn how to make a quilted butterfly.

Here are some things to remember when you follow directions.

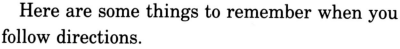

1. Read the directions before you begin.
2. Gather your materials. Be sure you have all the things you need before you start your work.
3. Read each step carefully and follow the steps in order.

Things you will need:

an 8½-inch by 11-inch
   piece of paper
a pencil
scissors
two 9-inch by 10-inch
   pieces of fabric
thread

a needle
cotton balls
glue
two buttons
two 5-inch pieces
   of ribbon

1. Fold the piece of paper in half. Starting at the fold, draw half of the butterfly. Cut on the lines you have drawn. Do not cut along the fold. Unfold the butterfly. You now have made a pattern.

2. Lay the pattern on top of the first piece of fabric. Trace the pattern of the butterfly onto the fabric and cut it out. Do the same thing with the second piece of fabric.

3. Put both pieces of fabric together with the right sides touching.

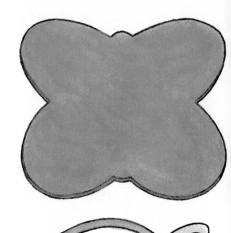

4. Cut a piece of thread about 24 inches long. Thread the needle and then knot the longer piece of thread.

5. Stitch the two pieces of fabric together. Leave openings for the stuffing on each wing. When the pieces have been stitched together, turn the butterfly right-side out.

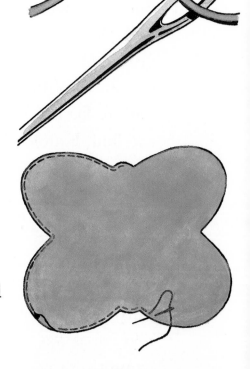

6. Stitch down the middle of the butterfly to make two wings.

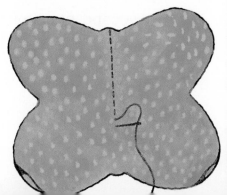

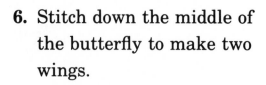

7. Stuff each wing with cotton balls. Stitch the open edges closed.

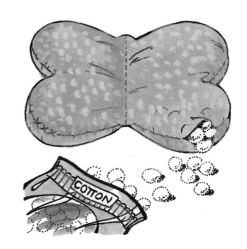

8. Glue two buttons onto the butterfly for its eyes. Glue the two pieces of ribbon onto the butterfly for its feelers.

Now you have made a quilted butterfly. You might want to sew a ribbon to your butterfly and hang it in your room. You could even give it to someone as a present.

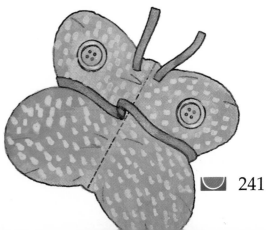

The Miser Who Wanted the Sun

by Jürg Obrist

Once there was a very rich man who was a miser. He lived in a huge house that had many treasures. He slept in a golden bed. He wore golden slippers.

No matter how much he owned, he still wanted more and more treasures. The more he collected, the more he wanted. "He loves gold," people said. "He would even like to own the sun if he could."

"Oh, yes," sighed the miser. "If only I could own the sun! It would make my robes shine like gold." Then he had an idea. What he could have was a robe, as bright and golden as the sun itself.

So he went to the tailor and ordered a golden
robe. The tailor shook his head. He had never
heard such a strange thing before.

"I'm not worried about the cost," the miser
said. "You can choose your payment from my
treasure room." The tailor agreed to make the
robe.

The tailor cut out the robe from the beautiful
golden cloth. The tailor's wife sewed the cloth.
The tailor's children, Tim and Lily, sewed on the
fine buttons and beautiful gems. They all worked
for days and days.

Soon the miser began to worry that the tailor
might take too many of his treasures. So, one by
one, he hid his treasures in another room.
"There's still plenty left for the tailor," he said,
and smiled to himself.

The tailor and his children brought the golden robe to the miser. The miser looked at it carefully. "Now you may choose your payment from my treasure room," he told them.

Inside the treasure room there was only one large chest. "The treasures must be in there," the tailor and his children thought. They opened it quickly, but the chest looked empty! Only a tiny golden thimble lay at the bottom.

"Is this our payment?" Tim asked angrily. "Don't worry, this chest will be useful," said Lily. She suddenly had an idea. Tim and Lily lifted the chest onto a cart. Then they pulled it home.

A few days later, Tim and Lily came back to see the miser. "We have heard that it is your greatest wish to own the sun," they said.

"The sun!" the miser sighed. "It's the only thing I still need for my collection of treasures."

"We know how to catch it for you," said Lily. "In return, we want to choose something from your house."

The miser was so excited, he agreed. "You may have whatever your hands can carry."

That evening, the miser watched Tim and Lily from his house, as they had told him to do. They pulled the empty treasure chest up the hill, behind which the sun set each day. At the top of the hill, they opened the lid and waited.

The sun began to set, right into the chest. The miser watched carefully as the last beam of light faded. Then the children quickly shut the lid and brought the chest back to the miser.

"You have certainly earned your payment," the miser said.

"All we want is your golden robe," said the children. They quickly took the robe and carried it home.

The miser had never felt so happy before. Now he was richer than ever! He looked forward to the next day when he could enjoy having the sun all to himself.

The next morning he woke early. He jumped to the window and saw that the sun was rising over the forest, just as it did every day.

"It can't be!" The miser was very angry. He ran to the chest and opened it. The chest was empty! Only the tiny golden thimble lay at the bottom. Now the miser understood that he had to enjoy the sun where it was, like everyone else.

Later that day, the miser went to the tailor and his family. This time, he brought them fair payment for their work. Then they gave him back the golden robe.

As he carried the robe home, it seemed to shine even brighter in the evening sun. "Everyone can share the sun," the miser said, "but no one has a golden robe like mine!"

1. What lesson did the miser learn?

2. Who taught the miser this lesson? How?

3. What did each of the people in the tailor's family do to make the robe?

4. Do you think the miser was happy at the end of the story? Why?

5. What made you know that the miser was not a fair man?

6. The miser was very rich, and he could buy anything he wanted. What lesson did the miser learn?

Think and Write

Prewrite

Think about how the story would have been different if the miser had wanted to own the moon.

Copy and complete the idea burst that follows with ways the miser might try to get the moon.

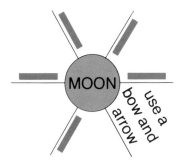

Draft

Write a story with the same characters as "The Miser Who Wanted the Sun," but have the miser want the moon intead of the sun. Create an interesting plan for him to get it. How might the tailor and his children help? Use your imagination.

Revise

Read your story over again very carefully. Make sure that it reads smoothly and that it fits together well. Does your story include enough details to make it interesting for your reader? Add to and fix your story to make it the best it can be.

Predict Outcomes

Look at the picture. What do you think is going to happen? Because you think you know what will happen, you can **predict** what a story about the picture will say. Good readers predict as they read.

What do you think the man in the picture might do next? Did you say that the man might mend his torn shirt? What clues make you think this? The clues are the torn shirt, the pins, needles, and thread.

You are predicting an outcome when you use the clues to tell what will happen next.

Read the paragraph below. Predict what Sarah might do. Then tell what clues helped you to think that.

Sarah had been saving pieces of cloth for nearly a year. Each scrap was placed in a bag, and now the bag was full. She had never let her sister, Rose, see what was in the bag. Now Sarah was going to begin.

What did you predict was going to happen? You may have thought that Sarah was going to make a quilt. The clues are the full bag and knowing that Sarah was going to begin doing something.

Sometimes authors do not give you all the clues in a story at one time, so your predictions may have to change. As you read, you get new clues that lead you to change your predictions. When you take new clues and put them together with what you already know, and then change your predictions, you are being a good reader.

Now read more about Sarah to see if she really will make a quilt.

As Sarah tied a pretty red ribbon around the bag of cloth scraps, she thought how surprised Rose would be when she opened her birthday present. Sarah had pretended that she was saving the scraps of cloth for herself, but now Rose would have enough cloth to make her first quilt.

Did you change your predictions? Why? As you read, remember to look for clues that help you make predictions about what might happen. Remember, also, to look for new clues and be ready to change your predictions.

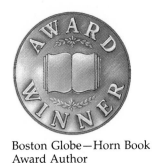

Folktales explain why things are the way they are. Read this folktale to find out how some people explain why spiders live in ceilings.

Why Spider Lives in Ceilings

retold by Joyce Cooper Arkhurst

adapted by Anne Maley

CHARACTERS

Storyteller 1	Elephant	Storyteller 2
Mother	Tortoise	Storyteller 3
Girl	Spider	
Hare	Leopard	

Storyteller 1: Once upon a time the rainy season came to the forest of West Africa, as it must come every year. This time there was more rain than ever before. Nobody had ever seen anything like it. The people in the villages were frightened.

Mother: *(excitedly)* Listen to the rain pounding on our roof! The water pours down with a roar like thunder! *(She opens the door and looks out.)* Water rushes everywhere, and the footpaths look like rivers!

Girl: *(sadly)* Look how the rain beats against the tree branches and tears off their leaves.

Mother: Let us close the door. There is no use looking outside. All we will see is rain, rain, rain!

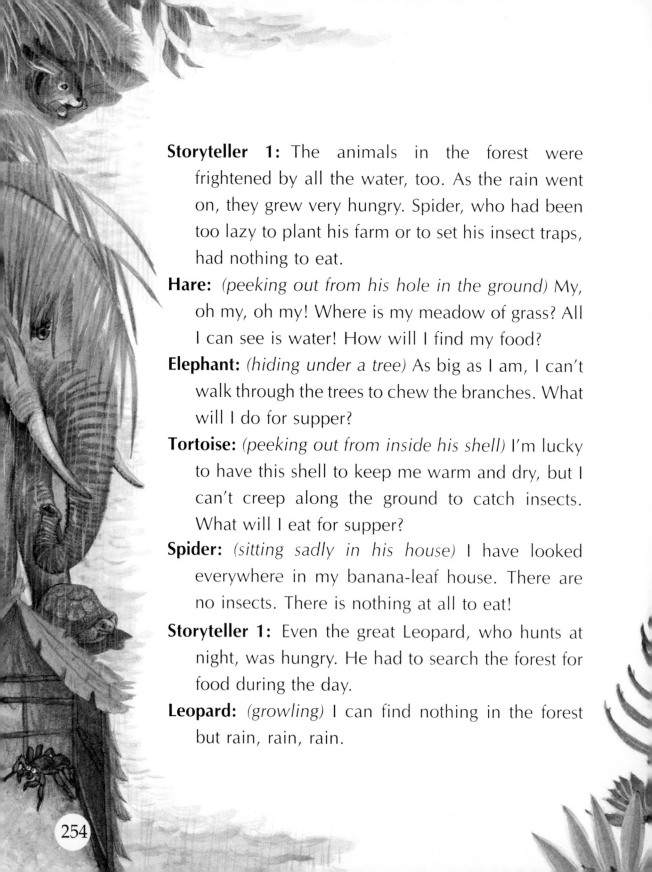

Storyteller 1: The animals in the forest were frightened by all the water, too. As the rain went on, they grew very hungry. Spider, who had been too lazy to plant his farm or to set his insect traps, had nothing to eat.

Hare: *(peeking out from his hole in the ground)* My, oh my, oh my! Where is my meadow of grass? All I can see is water! How will I find my food?

Elephant: *(hiding under a tree)* As big as I am, I can't walk through the trees to chew the branches. What will I do for supper?

Tortoise: *(peeking out from inside his shell)* I'm lucky to have this shell to keep me warm and dry, but I can't creep along the ground to catch insects. What will I eat for supper?

Spider: *(sitting sadly in his house)* I have looked everywhere in my banana-leaf house. There are no insects. There is nothing at all to eat!

Storyteller 1: Even the great Leopard, who hunts at night, was hungry. He had to search the forest for food during the day.

Leopard: *(growling)* I can find nothing in the forest but rain, rain, rain.

Storyteller 2: Then one afternoon, the rain stopped. Spider set out at once to look for something to eat. He went down the wide path that led to the river.

Leopard was hunting, too, with a hungry look in his eye. He walked quietly along the path that led to the river. That is how it happened that Spider and Leopard walked right into each other.

Usually, Leopard loves a fat and juicy supper. But today he thought even a small spider would taste good, so he stopped to chat and tried to look friendly.

Leopard: *(sweetly)* Good afternoon, Mr. Spider. How are you feeling after all this wet weather?

Storyteller 2: Spider was lazy, but he was clever, too. He knew at once that Leopard's voice was much too sweet.

255

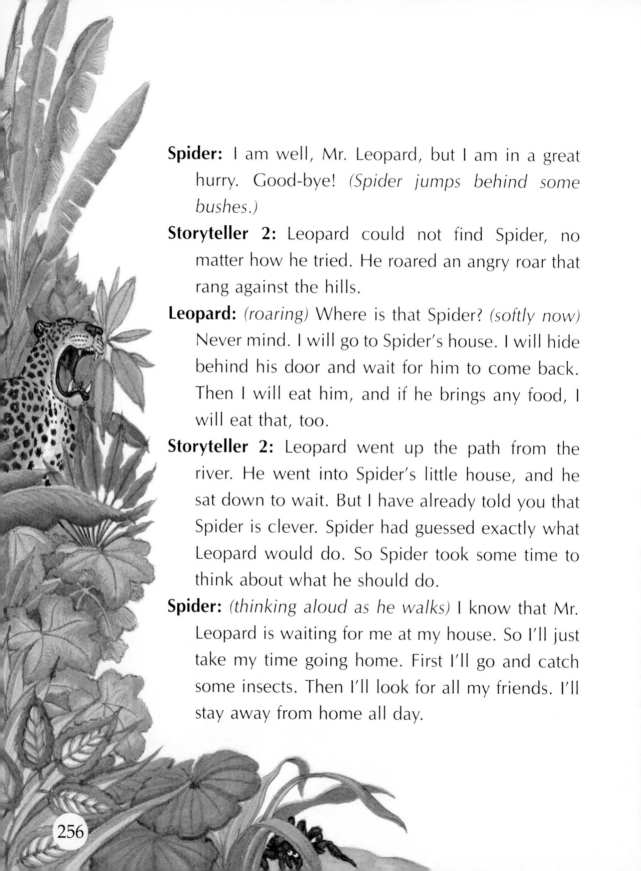

Spider: I am well, Mr. Leopard, but I am in a great hurry. Good-bye! *(Spider jumps behind some bushes.)*

Storyteller 2: Leopard could not find Spider, no matter how he tried. He roared an angry roar that rang against the hills.

Leopard: *(roaring)* Where is that Spider? *(softly now)* Never mind. I will go to Spider's house. I will hide behind his door and wait for him to come back. Then I will eat him, and if he brings any food, I will eat that, too.

Storyteller 2: Leopard went up the path from the river. He went into Spider's little house, and he sat down to wait. But I have already told you that Spider is clever. Spider had guessed exactly what Leopard would do. So Spider took some time to think about what he should do.

Spider: *(thinking aloud as he walks)* I know that Mr. Leopard is waiting for me at my house. So I'll just take my time going home. First I'll go and catch some insects. Then I'll look for all my friends. I'll stay away from home all day.

Storyteller 3: And that is what Spider did. Finally, it began to get dark. The sky filled with clouds, and once again the rain began to fall. At last Spider had to go home. So he went up the path that led past the river and near his little house made of banana leaves.

Spider: *(looking down at the ground)* I don't see Mr. Leopard's tracks. *(He listens hard.)* I don't hear Mr. Leopard's sounds. *(He looks all around.)* But I *know* Mr. Leopard is around here somewhere.

257

Storyteller 3: Even though Spider saw and heard nothing, he knew the ways of Leopard. So Spider kept walking down the path, humming to himself, just as if he were thinking of nothing. Suddenly he cried out.

Spider: *(shouting)* Hello, my banana-leaf house!

Storyteller 3: Nobody answered. Spider walked a little nearer. Still there was quiet.

Spider: *(loudly)* That's funny. My little house always answers me when I call it. I wonder what is wrong. *(He shouts again, with all his might.)* Hello, my banana-leaf house! How are you?

Storyteller 3: From deep inside the house came a small, high voice.

Leopard: *(speaking in a high little voice)* I am fine, Mr. Spider. Come on in.

Spider: *(laughing)* Ha, ha! Now I know where you are, Mr. Leopard, and you'll never catch me!

Storyteller 3: With that, Spider ran as quick as a flash through the window and up to the highest part of the ceiling. Leopard could not catch him even though he tried and tried. Spider was warm and dry and safe in the ceiling. I suppose that is why he decided to live there, and he is living there still!

1. How does this folktale explain why spiders live in ceilings?

2. Why did Spider and Leopard meet?

3. How did Spider trick Leopard into telling him where he was?

4. Which animal do you think was smarter, Spider or Leopard? Why?

5. How do you know that the water was very high?

6. Spider thought and planned carefully to solve his problem. How was this important to him?

Prewrite

Look back at how this story is told. A storyteller helps to move the story along, but basically the story is told by what the people and the animals say to each other. Think about a story that you might like to write, and how you could tell it using just the words that people say to one another.

Spiders in African Folktales

The play you just read was about another spider. It was taken from a West African folktale that told why spiders live in ceilings. Folktales often explain why something happened or how something was made.

In West Africa, the spider was known as Anansi. He was full of mischief, but very clever. He loved to eat, and hated to work.

In one Anansi story, Anansi was walking through the forest early one morning. He noticed a wonderful smell and remembered that it was a holiday. Anansi wondered how he would know which village would serve the best food. He thought and thought. Finally Anansi came up with a plan and called both his sons to him.

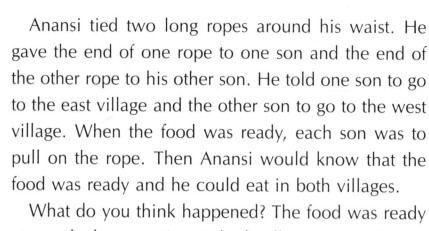

Anansi tied two long ropes around his waist. He gave the end of one rope to one son and the end of the other rope to his other son. He told one son to go to the east village and the other son to go to the west village. When the food was ready, each son was to pull on the rope. Then Anansi would know that the food was ready and he could eat in both villages.

What do you think happened? The food was ready at exactly the same time in both villages! Anansi's two sons each pulled hard on the rope, just as their father had told them. Anansi was pulled in both directions, but could go neither east nor west. The rope pulled tighter and tighter. Anansi's waist was squeezed thinner and thinner. Even today, some people still believe this is why spiders have thin waists.

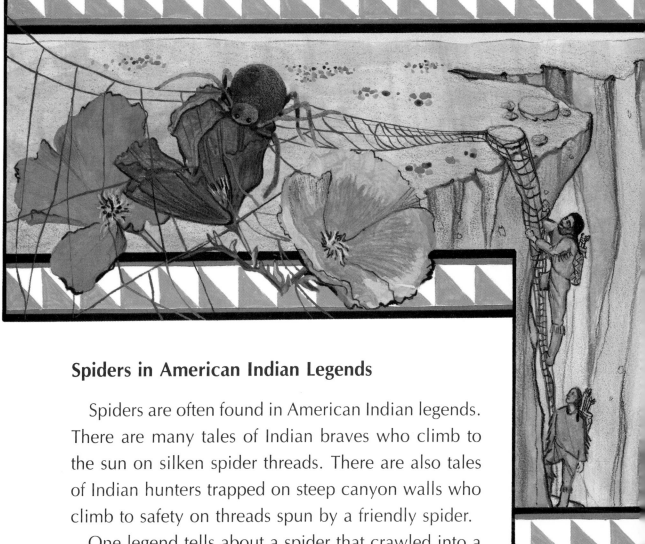

Spiders in American Indian Legends

Spiders are often found in American Indian legends. There are many tales of Indian braves who climb to the sun on silken spider threads. There are also tales of Indian hunters trapped on steep canyon walls who climb to safety on threads spun by a friendly spider.

One legend tells about a spider that crawled into a big clam shell. Two snails helped the spider turn the top half of the shell into the sky, and the bottom half into the Earth. Then the spider turned the two snails into the sun and the moon.

267

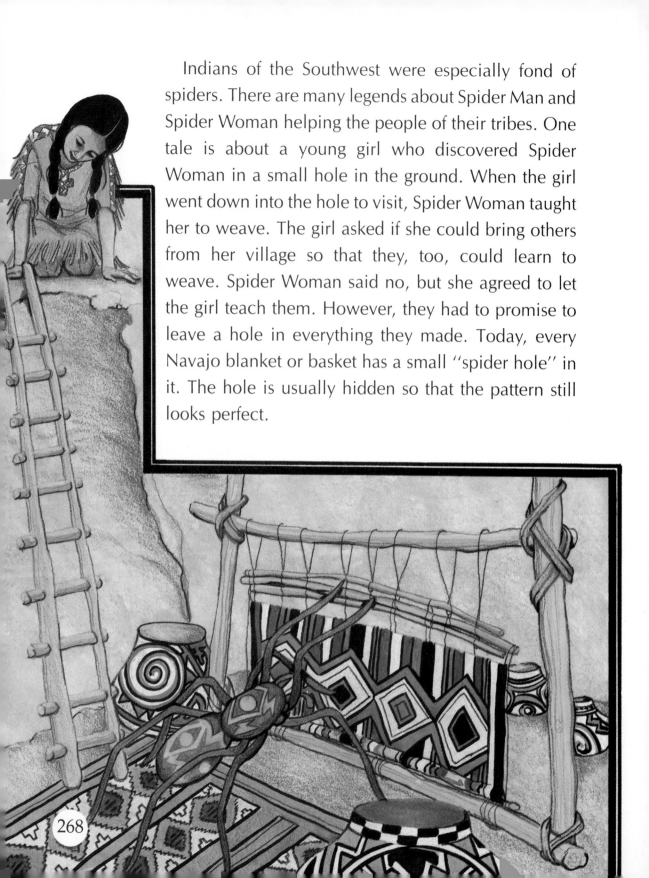

Indians of the Southwest were especially fond of spiders. There are many legends about Spider Man and Spider Woman helping the people of their tribes. One tale is about a young girl who discovered Spider Woman in a small hole in the ground. When the girl went down into the hole to visit, Spider Woman taught her to weave. The girl asked if she could bring others from her village so that they, too, could learn to weave. Spider Woman said no, but she agreed to let the girl teach them. However, they had to promise to leave a hole in everything they made. Today, every Navajo blanket or basket has a small "spider hole" in it. The hole is usually hidden so that the pattern still looks perfect.

Now that you have read folktales and stories that tell about spiders, you may want to learn about real spiders. Do spiders help or hurt people? How many different webs do spiders spin? Do all spiders live on land or can they survive underwater?

The next time you see a spider outside, look to see if it has a thin waist, like Anansi. Find out how this spider catches its food, and look to see what kind of web it has. Maybe this spider will spin a web just for you!

1. Who were the famous spiders we read about?

2. What part of the world did these legends and folktales come from?

3. Do you think that Anansi's idea was a good one? Why or why not?

4. What was the Indian hunters' problem in the story?

5. How do you know that Indians still think spiders are important?

6. Why do you think that people who lived long ago made up these tales?

Prewrite

You have learned new information about spiders. Think about the folktales and legends on spiders as you look at the story starters on page 271.

| Anansi the Spider is crawling over your shoulder . . |
| You meet Spiderman or Spiderwoman . . . |
| Your ideas . . . |

Draft

Using the starters above or your own ideas, write a tale or legend about a famous spider. Make sure you include yourself in the story. Spin a real tale!

Revise

Read your story to a classmate. Afterwards, think about the questions your teacher asks about your work. Make any changes that will improve your tale or legend.

Bar Graphs

Tim's science teacher asked the class to make a report on the different kinds of spiders they learned about. Tim wrote the first paragraph for his report. Read the paragraph.

My class learned about five different kinds of spiders. Seven people learned about the wolf spider. Two people learned about the crab spider. Three people learned about the water spider. One person learned about the grass spider, and nine people learned about the purse-web spider.

Then Tim's teacher helped him show the same information in a special drawing called a **bar graph.** Study the bar graph. Then look back to the paragraph. Decide which is the easier way to understand how many different spiders Tim's class studied.

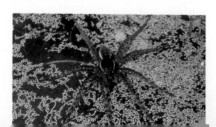

Look at the bar graph. The title tells what is being shown. The labels along the bottom name the kinds of spiders Tim's class studied. Look at the numerals along the left side. On this bar graph, the numerals show the number of children that studied about each kind of spider.

Next Tim decided to make a bar graph to show the different kinds of spider webs his class found. Read it to see how many different kinds of webs the children found.

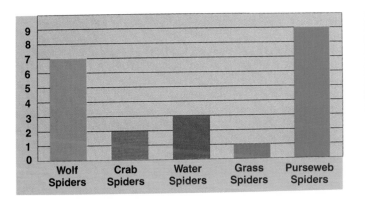
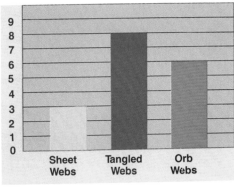

Find how many sheet webs the children found. The numeral on the left side shows that the children found three sheet webs. How many tangled webs did they find? The children found eight tangled webs. How many orb webs were found? The children found six orb webs.

Reading a bar graph is one way to get information. Bar graphs are sometimes easier to understand than a paragraph and help you find information quickly.

Textbook Application: Bar Graphs in Social Studies

A bar graph is often used in textbooks to help present some information. Read the following paragraph, bar graph, and questions from a social studies textbook. Then use the information on the bar graph to answer the questions.

Learning About Bar Graphs

What was the population (pop′yə·lā′shən) of the United States when it won its independence? Population is the number of people who live in a place. Soon after the United States was born, Americans decided to find out the population of their country. In 1790 they made a count, or census, of the population.

Americans learned many things from the first census. They learned that Virginia had the largest population. They learned that Delaware had the smallest population. They also found out which cities had the most people.

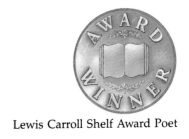

Seeds
by *Walter de la Mare*

The seeds I sowed—
For weeks unseen—
Have pushed up pygmy
Shoots of green;
So frail you'd think
The tiniest stone
Would never let
A glimpse be shown.
But no, a pebble
Near them lies,
At least a cherry stone
In size,
Which that mere sprout
Has heaved away,
To bask in sun,
And see the day.

What birthday gift did Sumi find to make Ojii Chan's heart sing?

Sumi's Special Happening

by Yoshiko Uchida

Before long, it would be December 5th, and Sumi (soo'mē) still did not have a birthday gift for Ojii Chan (ō·jē' chən).

Ojii Chan was Gonzaburo Oda (gən·zä' boo·rō ō'dä). He was the oldest person in the village, and one of Sumi's best friends.

Each year Sumi made him something for his birthday. This year, Mr. Oda was not having an ordinary birthday—he was going to be ninety-nine!

"What shall I give Ojii Chan for this very special birthday?" Sumi wondered.

"Do something to make his heart sing," Mr. Oda's housekeeper told Sumi. The village mayor told her, "If I were ninety-nine, I'm sure I would have all the things I needed. What I would want is a happening."

That night Sumi lay inside her heavy quilts and tried to think of an exciting happening she could bring into Ojii Chan's life. "What can I do?" she wondered. Soon she fell asleep, full of unanswered questions.

The next day was a Sunday. It was the day that Mr. Hattori (hä·tō'rē) always came to visit Father. Mr. Hattori lived in Kasa (kä'sä) Village beyond the wooded hills. Once a month he came on the red bus to spend an afternoon with Father.

Today Mr. Hattori had much to tell. "I am the new one-man fire department of Kasa Village," he said proudly. "I am in charge of the fire truck."

"That is a big job," Father said. "You are able to drive such a truck?"

"Well, it is not exactly a truck," Mr. Hattori explained. "It is an old jeep made to look like a fire truck. We carry some fire-fighting equipment. It is a wonderful sight."

"Does it have a siren?" asked Sumi's brother Taro (tä'rō).

"It does indeed," Mr. Hattori nodded, "and bells—it has many bells."

Sumi wondered what it would be like to ride in such a jeep. In Sugi (sōō'jē) Village no one even owned a car. There was no bus. Anyone could walk from one end of the village to the other in fifteen minutes.

Suddenly, the happening Sumi was searching for popped into her head. Before she could even think of a polite way to ask, she was begging Mr. Hattori for a ride on this wonderful jeep.

"It's not for me," she explained. "It's for Ojii Chan." Quickly she told how she needed a very special happening for Mr. Gonzaburo Oda on his ninety-ninth birthday on December 5th. Sumi was quite sure he had never ridden on a jeep before. Surely he had never in his life ridden on a fire engine jeep.

Mr. Hattori listened to Sumi. He wondered if such a thing would be all right for the one-man fire department of Kasa Village to do. Then he smiled and hit the table with his hand.

"I shall do it," he said. "I will come to take Mr. Oda for a ride. I shall give you *all* a ride such as you have never had in your lives I will help you give Mr. Oda a day he will never forget!"

"*Banzai!*" (bän'zī) Sumi and her brother Taro shouted together. They could hardly wait for December 5th to come.

Later Sumi told Mr. Mayor of the happening she had decided upon. He shook her hand as though he were giving her an award.

"That is exactly right, exactly right!" he cried. "A happening such as that will surely warm his heart." Then he told Sumi to be sure that their ride ended at the school. "I shall have a happening of my own for Mr. Oda," he said.

When Sumi woke up on December 5th, she saw that it had snowed overnight. Snow was still falling from the sky. How would Mr. Hattori ever get his jeep over the hills with all this snow?

"It's snowing!" Sumi cried, but Mr. Hattori came at the time he had promised. He was wearing a big coat. His cheeks were red from the cold.

Sumi and Taro ran outside. There in front of their house was a red jeep. It was so red, it looked like a big apple. A ladder was tied to its side. Buckets hung from the rear. From a rope strung along its sides hung many bells of every size and shape. First Mr. Hattori gave the rope a tug. The bells rang in the snowy stillness. Sumi clapped her hands.

Next, Mr. Hattori pushed the big horn. It sounded like an angry moose. Then he pulled on a chain that made the siren scream.

Taro could wait no longer. Shouting happily, he climbed onto the fire engine jeep. No one in the world could have pulled him off. Mother and Father heard the noise and hurried outside with the children's coats and hats.

Mother and Father just had time to bow and greet Mr. Hattori. Then, with a great, loud roar, Mr. Hattori started the jeep. He hurried off with Sumi and Taro to Mr. Oda's house.

"Ojii Chan, Ojii Chan!" Sumi shouted as she streaked into his house. "Happy birthday! *Omedeto!* (ō·me·de'tō) Put on your warmest coat and hat. I have a birthday surprise for you!"

"A surprise?" Ojii Chan asked in a thin voice.

"Hurry, Ojii Chan," Sumi begged. Mr. Oda put on his great black cape and his beaver hat. Sumi could hardly wait!

Mr. Oda saw the bright red fire engine jeep at his gate. His mouth fell open into a great "O." He blinked his eyes as though he couldn't believe what he saw.

Mr. Hattori bowed deeply and rang all the bells. Taro squeezed the horn and shouted, "Happy birthday, Ojii Chan!"

"We're taking you for a ride," Sumi said, tugging at Ojii Chan's sleeve. "This is my birthday present. It's a special happening so you won't ever forget your ninety-ninth birthday."

Ojii Chan shook his head. He smiled at the wonderful sight in front of him. He was so pleased he didn't know what to do.

"We shall circle the rice fields of Sugi Village three times. Then we shall go to the village school," Mr. Hattori said. Carefully he helped Mr. Oda into the jeep. Then he shouted, "Now, let us go!" Away they roared down the road like a noisy red bull.

The one-man fire department of Kasa Village made the siren scream and the bells ring. They rumbled past snow-covered fields. By the second time they went around the village, people came outside. They stood in front of their houses to see what all the noise was about.

"It's Ojii Chan's birthday!" Sumi and Taro shouted together at all the wondering faces. When they heard, the villagers laughed and waved and shouted, *"Banzai! Banzai!"*

Many of the village children followed the noisy red jeep. At last it reached the school. The yard was already filled with the laughing, shouting children, and many of their parents.

Mr. Mayor hurried out to greet them. *"Omedeto!* Congratulations!" he said, smiling and bowing to Mr. Oda. "Please step inside and warm yourself."

They all went inside. Sumi saw that the mayor had made a fine happening of his own. His wife had come with him. She had set up a table covered with a red and white cloth.

On the table were plates heaped with food. The news of Mr. Oda's birthday had spread quickly. Now other villagers came, bringing tins of crackers, fruit, and anything they could find in their homes. Sumi's mother and father came carrying their gifts.

"It's a big party!" Sumi said happily.

"It's the best thing that's happened all year," Taro added.

Mr. Oda was so happy he sniffled into his big white handkerchief. Mr. Mayor stood up and told Mr. Oda how happy he was that they had all been able to celebrate his ninety-ninth birthday with him. He told how Sumi's happening had given him the idea for this party.

Everyone agreed that it was the nicest happening to have come along in a long, long time. They came to pat Sumi on the head. They told her how pleased they were that she'd had such a fine idea. Ojii Chan himself told her that he'd never had a finer birthday in all his life.

When it was time to go home, Mr. Oda thanked everyone who had come. Then he returned happily to the fire engine jeep for the ride home.

"Blow your horn, Mr. Fire Department!" Mr. Oda called out. "Blow your siren! This time *I* am going to ring your bells." He reached for the rope strung with the bells and rang them just as hard as he could.

"Ojii Chan, *banzai!*" everyone shouted. In a blaze of wonderful noise they roared back to Mr. Oda's house.

They made such a loud noise that Ojii Chan's housekeeper came rushing to the gate. "Are you all right?" she asked him.

"Of course I'm all right," Mr. Oda said. "I have just had more fun today than I have had in a very long time."

The old housekeeper nodded. "I can tell," she said. "It is there for all to see on your face." Then she smiled at Sumi. "The heart is singing, little one," she said. "You gave him the best gift of all."

1. What was Sumi's birthday gift to Ojii Chan?

2. Why did Sumi want to give Ojii Chan a special birthday gift?

3. How did Mr. Hattori's visit help Sumi?

4. How do you think Sumi felt at the end of the story? Why?

5. When did you know that Ojii Chan liked his birthday gifts?

6. The best gift is one from the heart. Why do you know that Ojii Chan liked Sumi's gift the best?

Thinking About "Windows"

In this unit, you learned that there are different kinds of windows. Some windows can show you what things were like long ago. Other windows can help people see themselves more clearly.

You read old tales about a miser, a clever spider, and three lazy brothers. These old stories have been told over and over again by many people. You also read stories about how old quilts can tell stories about the past. What can you learn from legends and folktales?

Sumi looked into the window of her own heart in order to predict what would make Ojii Chan happy. Were her predictions correct?

As you read other stories, look for those that are windows to the past. Look also for those stories that have different kinds of windows.

1. How are the characters in "Sam Johnson and the Blue Ribbon Quilt," "The Miser Who Wanted the Sun," and "The Buried Treasure" alike? What did they learn?

2. How are the selections "The Great American Quilt" and "Famous Spiders" alike? How are they different?

3. How are the miser, Tim and Lily, Spider, and Leopard alike? How are they different? Why?

4. Both Sam Johnson and Sumi had problems. What were these problems, and how were they solved?

5. If you could learn more about one of the characters in this unit, which character would you choose? Why?

Glossary

The glossary is a special dictionary for this book. The glossary tells you how to spell a word, how to pronounce it, and what the word means. Often the word is used in a sentence. Different forms of the word may follow the sentence. If one of the different forms is used in the book, then that form may be used in the sentence.

A blue box ■ at the end of the entry tells you that an illustration is given for that word.

The following abbreviations are used throughout the glossary: *n.,* noun; *v.,* verb; *adj.,* adjective; *adv.,* adverb; *interj.,* interjection; *prep.,* preposition; *conj.,* conjunction; *pl.,* plural; *sing.,* singular.

An accent mark (′) is used to show which syllable receives the most stress. For example, in the word *granite* [gran′ it], the first syllable receives the most stress. Sometimes in words of three or more syllables, there is also a lighter mark to show that a syllable receives a lighter stress. For example, in the word *helicopter* [hel′ ə ·kop′ tər], the first syllable has the most stress, and the third syllable has lighter stress.

The symbols used to show how each word is pronounced are explained in the "Pronunciation Key" on the next page.

Pronunciation Key*

a	add, map	m	move, seem	u	up, done
ā	ace, rate	n	nice, tin	û(r)	burn, term
â(r)	care, air	ng	ring, song	yo͞o	fuse, few
ä	palm, father	o	odd, hot	v	vain, eve
b	bat, rub	ō	open, so	w	win, away
ch	check, catch	ô	order, jaw	y	yet, yearn
d	dog, rod	oi	oil, boy	z	zest, muse
e	end, pet	ou	pout, now	zh	vision, pleasure
ē	equal, tree	o͝o	took, full	ə	the schwa,
f	fit, half	o͞o	pool, food		an unstressed
g	go, log	p	pit, stop		vowel representing
h	hope, hate	r	run, poor		the sound spelled
i	it, give	s	see, pass	a	in *above*
ī	ice, write	sh	sure, rush	e	in *sicken*
j	joy, ledge	t	talk, sit	i	in *possible*
k	cool, take	th	thin, both	o	in *melon*
l	look, rule	th̶	this, bathe	u	in *circus*

*Adapted entries, the Pronunciation Key, and the Short Key that appear on the following pages are reprinted from *HBJ School Dictionary.* Copyright ©1985 by Harcourt Brace Jovanovich, Inc. Reprinted by permission of Harcourt Brace Jovanovich, Inc.

A

aeronaut [âr′ə·nôt] *n.* A person who flies an aircraft, especially a balloon: The *aeronaut* landed the hot-air balloon on the grass. ■

alarm [ə·lärm′] *v.* **alarmed, alarming** To upset: The loud noise *alarmed* the baby. *syns.* frighten, upset

among [ə·mung′] *prep.* In a group of: His poems were *among* the best in the book.

ancestor [an′ses·tər] *n., pl.* **ancestors** A person in one's family who lived earlier: My father's *ancestors* were from China.

arch [ärch′] *n., pl.* **arches** A rounded piece of material over an open place: There was a stone *arch* over the gate.

arrange [ə·rānj′] *v.* **arranged** To put in a certain order: We *arranged* the books on the shelf. *syns.* sort, place, classify

artistic [är·tis′tik] *adj.* Showing skill in music or any art: My *artistic* sister can draw beautiful pictures and can also play the piano well.

asleep [ə·slēp′] **1** *adj.* Sleeping: Marty is *asleep* in the chair. *syns.* sleeping, napping **2** *adv.* Into sleep: Karen fell *asleep*.

attach [ə·tach′] *v.* **attached, attaching** To connect: Joe *attached* the string to the kite. *syn.* fasten

attack [ə·tak′] *v.* **attacked, attacking** To set upon with force; begin a fight with: The lion was *attacking* the deer. *syn.* assault

audience [ô′dē·əns] *n., pl.* **audiences** A group of people who come to listen to or watch something, as a concert or play: The *audience* liked the band music. *syn.* listeners

author [ô′thər] *n., pl.* **authors**
A person who has written a book, story, song, or play: The *author* placed the book she had written on the desk. *syn.* writer

award [ə·wôrd′] *n., pl.* **awards**
A prize: Her painting got an *award. syn.* prize

awning [ô′ning] *n., pl.*
awnings A cover, often made of canvas, used over a window or door for protection from sun or rain: The *awning* kept the room cool and dark. ▪

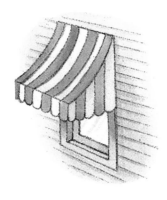

B

badger [baj′ər] *n., pl.* **badgers**
A small animal with short legs, a wide back, and thick fur: The *badger* came out to find food. ▪

bicycle [bī′sik·əl] *n., pl.*
bicycles A machine with two large wheels and pedals, on which a person rides: Tanya rode her *bicycle* to school.

bore [bôr] *v.* **bored, boring** To make tired by being uninteresting or dull: The long play was *boring* the people. *syn.* tire

bravo [brä′vō] *interj.* What people call out when someone has done a good job: The people shouted *"Bravo!"* when the singer finished the song.

a	add	o	odd	oi	oil
ā	ace	ō	open	ou	pout
â	care	ô	order	ng	ring
ä	palm	o͝o	took	th	thin
e	end	o͞o	pool	th	this
ē	equal	u	up	zh	vision
i	it	û	burn		
ī	ice	yo͞o	fuse		

ə = { a in *above*   e in *sicken*   i in *possible*
      o in *melon*   u in *circus* }

burro [bûr′ō] *n., pl.* **burros** An animal like a small donkey, used for riding or carrying things: The *burro* carried the heavy bags. *syn.* donkey ■

bury [ber′ē] *v.* **buried, burying** To put into the ground: The dog *buried* the bone.

C

cactus [kak′təs] *n., pl.* **cactuses** or **cacti** A desert plant covered with sharp spines: A *cactus* does not need much water.

camera [kam′(ə·)rə] *n., pl.* **cameras** A device used for taking pictures: My *camera* was broken, so I took no pictures.

canvas [kan′vəs] *n., pl.* **canvases** A heavy cloth on which people paint pictures: The artist filled the *canvas* with bright colors.

canyon [kan′yən] *n., pl.* **canyons** A narrow, deep valley with steep walls: The river cut a *canyon* through the rock. *syns.* valley, gorge

caught [kôt] *v.* Past tense of catch: I did not know she was behind me and was *caught* by surprise. *syn.* captured

ceiling [sē′ling] *n., pl.* **ceilings** The top side of a room: The *ceilings* are nine feet high in our house.

census [sen′səs] *n.* A counting of people: After the *census* was taken, we knew how many people lived in our town.

charcoal [chär′kōl] *n.* A black material made by burning wood, which may be used for drawing or for heat: The artist drew a picture with *charcoal.* ■

charge [chärj] *v.* **charged, charging** To ask for payment for something: They are *charging* ten dollars for dinner. *syn.* price

chuckle [chuk′əl] **1** *n., pl.* **chuckles** A soft laugh: Becky heard a *chuckle* coming from the porch. **2** *v.* **chuckled, chuckling** To laugh softly: Sammy *chuckled* when he heard the joke. *syns.* laugh, giggle

clever [klev′ər] *adj.* Smart; quick at thinking and solving problems: Cal was very *clever* to think of that idea. *syn.* cunning

cloth [klôth] *n.* A material such as cotton or wool: We found a piece of pretty blue *cloth* for my dress. *syns.* fabric, textile, material

collection [kə·lek′shən] *n.* Things brought together for study or for saving: He showed me his stamp *collection.*

D

dawn [dôn] *n.* The first light of day: At camp, we got up at *dawn. syns.* daybreak, sunrise

delicious [di·lish′əs] *adj.* Having a very good taste: Jason made *delicious* pancakes for breakfast. *syn.* tasty

department [di·pärt′mənt] *n., pl.* **departments** A part of a business, school, or government: Mrs. Cordero is the head of the School *Department.*

desert [dez′ərt] *n., pl.* **deserts** A dry, sand-covered region where few plants grow: It took two days to cross the *desert.*

a	add	o	odd	oi	oil
ā	ace	ō	open	ou	pout
â	care	ô	order	ng	ring
ä	palm	o͝o	took	th	thin
e	end	o͞o	pool	th	this
ē	equal	u	up	zh	vision
i	it	û	burn		
ī	ice	yo͞o	fuse		

ə = { a in *above*　e in *sicken*　i in *possible*
　　　 o in *melon*　u in *circus*

design [di·zīn'] **1** *n., pl.*
designs A plan or sketch to
be used as a pattern for
making something: She
looked for a *design* to paint
on the walls. *syn.* plan **2** *v.*
designed, designing To
make plans for making
something: He will *design*
new scenery for the play.
syns. plan, devise

diary [dī'·(ə·)rē] *n.* A person's
record of what happens
every day: He forgot to
write in his *diary* this week.

disappoint [dis'ə·point'] *v.*
disappointed, disappointing
To make unhappy because
something did or did not
happen: I was *disappointed*
when I lost the race. *syn.* let
down

E

---

easel [ē'zəl] *n., pl.* **easels** A
folding frame with three
legs, often used for holding
an artist's work: The artist

set up an *easel* and began to
draw. ■

eighty-six [ā'tē siks] *n., adj.*
Six more than eighty,
written 86: We have
eighty-six children in our
school.

encore [än(g)'kôr'] *interj.* A
call asking performers to
perform again: *"Encore,
encore!"* the people shouted
after the piano solo. *syns.*
again.

enemy [en'ə·mē] *n., pl.*
enemies A person or animal
that tries to harm another:
The mouse tried to get away
from its *enemy. syn.* foe

engine [en'jin] *n., pl.* **engines**
A machine that uses energy
to do work, such as turning
wheels: A car *engine* runs
on gas. *syn.* motor

equipment [i·kwip′mənt] *n.*
Something used for a certain
purpose: I have the
equipment we need to fix the
car. *syns.* supplies, provisions

exclaim [iks·klām′] *v.*
exclaimed, exclaiming To cry
out with anger or surprise:
"Oh no!" *exclaimed* Pete.

exist [ig·zist′] *v.* to be:
Dragons do not *exist* in the
real world. *syns.* live, be

F

fabric [fab′rik] *n.* A material
such as cloth or silk: His
shirt was made of silk *fabric.*
syns. cloth, material

fair [fâr] *adj.* **fairness** *n.* A
way of not favoring one
above another: He showed
fairness when giving the
prizes. *syns.* even, just

fiction [fik′shən] *n.* Stories
that have been made up:
The story "All About
Sammy" is *fiction.*

flexi-kite [fleks′ə·kīt] *n., pl.*
flexi-kites A type of kite

without a frame: The
flexi-kite flew over the
trees. ■

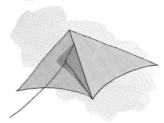

flood [flud] *n., pl.* **floods** A
great flow of water: The rain
brought on a *flood.*

fly [flī] *v.* **flew, flown, flying**
1 To move through the air:
Birds *fly. syn.* soar **2** To
cause to move through the
air: Have you ever *flown* an
airplane?

folktale [fōk′tāl] *n., pl.* **folktales** An old story handed
down through the years by
a group of people: *Little Red
Riding Hood* is a French *folktale.*

a	add	o	odd	oi	oil
ā	ace	ō	open	ou	pout
â	care	ô	order	ng	ring
ä	palm	o͝o	took	th	thin
e	end	o͞o	pool	th	this
ē	equal	u	up	zh	vision
i	it	û	burn		
ī	ice	yo͞o	fuse		

ə = { a in *above*, e in *sicken*, i in *possible*, o in *melon*, u in *circus* }

formation [for·mā′shən] *n., pl.*
formations Something made
into a certain shape: We saw
two rock *formations* that
looked like bridges in the
desert.

fortune [fôr′chən] *n., pl.*
fortunes A lot of money: He
made a *fortune* when he sold
his business. *syn.* wealth

forty [fôr′tē] *n.* Thirty plus
ten, written 40: I counted
forty chairs.

friendship [frend′ship′] *n., pl.*
friendships The state of
being friends: Without your
friendship, I would be lonely.

frighten [frīt′(ə)n] *v.*
frightened, frightening To
scare: Being alone *frightened*
the child. *syns.* scare, alarm,
terrify

fruit [frōōt] *n., pl.* **fruits** A
part of a flowering plant
that can be eaten: Apples
are my favorite kind of *fruit.*
syn. produce

fuddy-duddy [fud′ē dud′ē] *n.,
pl.* **fuddy-duddies** Someone
who has no new ideas: They
called him a *fuddy-duddy*

because he would not read
any new books.

G

gem [jem] *n., pl.* A cut and
polished stone: The green
gem was put into a ring.
syns. jewel, stone

gentle [jen′təl] *adj.* **gently** *adv.*
Kindly or soft: He touched
the kitten *gently. syns.* mild,
soft

gila woodpecker [hē′lə
wood′pek′ər] *n., pl.* **gila
woodpeckers** A desert bird
with a sharp bill for making
holes in cactuses: The *gila
woodpecker* has a strong bill.

gondola [gon′də·lə] *n., pl.*
gondolas A basket that
hangs from a hot-air
balloon: People can ride
in a balloon's *gondola.* ■

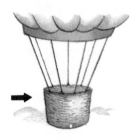

granite [gran'it] *n.* A hard rock, often used as a building material: The building was made from blocks of *granite*.

graph [graf] *n., pl.* **graphs** A diagram used to show information: My mother keeps *graphs* to show how tall I am. *syns.* chart, diagram

H

half [haf] *n., pl.* **halves** Either of two equal parts into which something can be divided: Ken can have *half* of the apple.

halfway [haf'wā'] *adj.* In the middle, between two points: Your house is *halfway* between my house and the school. *syns.* midway, center

handkerchief [hang'kər·chif] *n., pl.* **handkerchiefs** A small piece of cloth used to wipe the face and nose: My uncle always carries a white *handkerchief* in his pocket.

handlebar [han'dəl·bär'] *n., pl.* **handlebars** A bar used to steer, as on a bicycle: Marvin held on to the bicycle's *handlebars*.

happiness [hap'ē·nis] *n.* A state of being pleased and contented: The girl felt great *happiness* in knowing she had won the race. *syns.* joy, delight

harvest [här'vist] *n., pl.* **harvests** The gathering and bringing in of a crop: The farmer was glad he had a good *harvest* this year.

haunted [hôn'tid] *adj.* Visited by ghosts: My brother said the old house on the corner was *haunted*.

a	add	o	odd	oi	oil
ā	ace	ō	open	ou	pout
â	care	ô	order	ng	ring
ä	palm	o͝o	took	th	thin
e	end	o͞o	pool	t͟h	this
ē	equal	u	up	zh	vision
i	it	û	burn		
ī	ice	yo͞o	fuse		

ə = { a in *above*   e in *sicken*   i in *possible*
      o in *melon*   u in *circus* }

hedge [hej] *n., pl.* **hedges** A fence formed by bushes planted close together: The horse jumped over the *hedge* and ran away. ■

helmet [hel'mit] *n., pl.* **helmets** A hard covering worn to protect the head: She wears a *helmet* when she goes roller skating.

honor [on'ər] *n.* Respect: The people gave great *honor* to their hero.

hopeful [hōp'fəl] *adj.* **hopefully** *adv.* Having a feeling that what one wants may happen: "I want to be famous when I grow up," said Jim *hopefully*.

hospital [hos'pi·təl] *n., pl.* **hospitals** A place where sick or hurt people are cared for: Doctor Lester works in that *hospital*.

hundred [hun'drid] *n., pl.* **hundreds** *adj.* Ninety plus ten, written 100: There are *hundreds* of flowers in the fields.

I

illustrate [il'ə·strāt'] *v.* **illustrated, illustrating** To draw pictures for books: Mrs. Shaw writes books, and Mr. Shaw *illustrates* them. *syn.* draw

illustration [il'ə·strā'shən] *n., pl.* **illustrations** A picture in a book: The *illustrations* were done in bright colors. *syn.* picture

image [im'ij] *n., pl.* **images** A picture such as is formed by a lens: The *image* is shown on the screen. *syn.* picture

imagination [i·maj'ə·nā'shən] *n.* The power to picture something in the mind: The girl used her *imagination* to tell stories to the children.

independence [in'di·pen'dəns] *n.* Freedom: Many people like to have a feeling of *independence*.

insect [in′sekt] *n., pl.* **insects**
A small animal with six legs
and usually two pairs of
wings: Flies are *insects. syn.*
bug

interview [in′t r·vyoo′] *n., pl.*
interviews A meeting in
which one person gets
information from another:
The woman on the news
had an *interview* with the
contest winner.

invention [in·ven′·shən] *n., pl.*
inventions Something made
for the first time: We saw
several *inventions* in the
museum. *syn.* creation

inventor [in·ven′tər] *n., pl.*
inventors A person who
makes something no one has
made before: The *inventor*
made a new kind of electric
light.

J

jade [jād] *n.* A hard stone,
usually green, used as a
gem: He wanted a ring
made of *jade.*

K

knot [not] *n.* A fastening
made by tying ropes
together: He made a *knot* in
the rope to hold the dog. ■

a	add	o	odd	oi	oil
ā	ace	ō	open	ou	pout
â	care	ô	order	ng	ring
ä	palm	o͝o	took	th	thin
e	end	o͞o	pool	th	this
ē	equal	u	up	zh	vision
i	it	û	burn		
ī	ice	yo͞o	fuse		

ə = { a in *above* e in *sicken* i in *possible*
      o in *melon* u in *circus*

313

L

landscape [land′skāp′] *n., pl.* **landscapes 1** An area of land as seen from a certain point: I could look at this *landscape* all day. **2** A picture showing such a scene: Tony drew a beautiful *landscape.*

language [lang′gwij] *n.* A means of expressing thoughts and ideas: Some brothers and sisters make up their own *language.*

lawn [lôn] *n., pl.* **lawns** A piece of land covered with short grass: The children are playing on the *lawn. syn.* grass

layer [lā′ər] *n., pl.* **layers** One covering or thickness: We wore three *layers* of clothes to keep warm.

lazy [lā′zē] *adj.* Not willing to work: Ellie didn't do her homework because she was *lazy.*

legend [lej′ənd] *n., pl.* **legends** A story that has been passed down over many years, believed by many to be partly true: The story of Paul Bunyan is a famous American *legend.*

limestone [līm′stōn′] *n.* A kind of rock: They found pieces of *limestone* on the hill next to the beach.

M

marble [mär′bəl] *n.* A hard limestone in many colors, used especially in building: The windowsill was made of *marble.*

material [mə·tir′ē·əl] *n., pl.* **materials** That from which something is made: We have all the *materials* we need to make the dress. *syns.* fabric, textile

mesa [mā′sə] *n., pl.* **mesas** A hill with a flat top and steep sides: They camped on top of the *mesa.* ■

message [mes′ij] *n., pl.*
messages News or other
communication sent to
another pesron: Jane sent
me important *messages* in the
mail.

mischief [mis′chif] *n.* Behavior
that can cause trouble: John
had *mischief* in his eyes, so I
knew I had to watch him
carefully.

miser [mī′zər] *n., pl.* **misers** A
person who saves money
because he or she loves it:
The *miser* loved to count his
money.

muscle [mus′əl] *n., pl.* **muscles**
A part of the body that
makes the body move: My
muscles grew stronger when
I exercised.

musical [myoo′zi·kəl] *adj.*
Having to do with music:
Arlene is very *musical;* she
plays both drums and horns.

musician [myoo·zish′ən] *n., pl.*
musicians A person who is
skilled in music: My mother
is a fine *musician.*

N

neither [nē′thər *or* nī′thər]
adj., pron. Not either: *Neither*
of the boys wants to leave.

nervous [nûr′vəs] *adj.* Feeling
upset or very excited: Many
people are *nervous* before
taking a test. *syns.* tense,
uneasy

ninety-nine [nīn′tē nīn] *n., adj.*
One less than one hundred,
written 99. Darcy counted
ninety-nine stores.

ninety-ninth [nīn′tē nīnth] *adj.*
The one in order before one
hundredth: This was the
ninety-ninth year the band
had played.

novelty [nov′əl·tē] *n., pl.*
novelties A new or unusual
thing: I bought the game at
a *novelty* store.

a	add	o	odd	oi	oil
ā	ace	ō	open	ou	pout
â	care	ô	order	ng	ring
ä	palm	oo	took	th	thin
e	end	ōo	pool	th	this
ē	equal	u	up	zh	vision
i	it	û	burn		
ī	ice	yoo	fuse		

ə = { a in *above* e in *sicken* i in *possible*
      { o in *melon* u in *circus*

315

O

o'clock [ə·klok'] *adv.* Of the clock: Meet me here at nine *o'clock.*

orchard [ôr'chərd] *n., pl.* **orchards** A large group of trees grown for their fruit: The farmer tended her apple *orchard* with great care. *syn.* grove ■

ordinary [ôr'də·ner'ē] *adj.* Not special: It was an *ordinary* van like all the others in the park. *syns.* common, usual

P

pantomime [pan'tə·mīm'] *n.* A kind of acting that tells a story through actions rather than words: Marcel Marceau is one of the greatest actors of *pantomime.*

patchwork [pach'wûrk] *adj.* Patterns of cloth in different colors or shapes sewed together in a design: That *patchwork* quilt has been in my family for many years.

pattern [pat'ərn] *n., pl.* **patterns** A design of shapes or colors: That flowered cloth has a pretty *pattern.*

payment [pā'mənt] *n.* Something, usually money, given in exchange for things or work: Iris got five dollars as *payment* for cleaning the yard.

pedal [ped'(ə)l] *v.* **pedaled, pedaling** To move by pushing pedals with the feet: Angie *pedaled* her bicycle over to my house.

perform [pər·fôrm'] *v.* **performed, performing 1** To do: I will *perform* my job well. *syn.* do **2** To present an artistic skill, such as acting or singing: Mr. Ling will *perform* in the show.

phonograph [fō′nə·graf′] *n., pl.*
phonographs A machine that
plays records: The school
bought two new *phonographs*
for our classroom. *syn.*
record player ■

photograph [fō′tə·graf′] **1** *n.,*
pl. **photographs** A picture
taken with a camera: Did
you see the *photographs* of
Julio? *syns.* picture, snapshot
2 *v.* **photographed,**
photographing To take
pictures with a camera: She
went to the zoo to
photograph the animals.

population [pop′yə·lā′shən] *n.*
The number of people living
in a place: The *population* of
our town grows every year.
syns. people, inhabitants

pottery [pot′ər·ē] *n.* Things,
such as pots, made of clay
and hardened by heat: Many

people wanted to buy the
beautiful *pottery.* ■

powerful [pou′ər·fəl] *adj.*
Having great ability to do
something: The *powerful*
storm tore the trees down.

practice [prak′tis] *n., pl.*
practices An action done
many times in order to
improve one's skills: We have
singing *practice* every
Wednesday.

present [pri·zent′] *v.*
presented, presenting To
give to: Millie *presented* an
award to the winner. *syns.*
offer, give

a	add	o	odd	oi	oil
ā	ace	ō	open	ou	pout
â	care	ô	order	ng	ring
ä	palm	o͝o	took	th	thin
e	end	o͞o	pool	th	this
ē	equal	u	up	zh	vision
i	it	û	burn		
ī	ice	yo͞o	fuse		

ə = { a in *above*   e in *sicken*   i in *possible*
      { o in *melon*   u in *circus*

317

president [prez'ə·dent] *n., pl.*
presidents The person who
acts as head of a club or
group: The *president* asked
the people to take their
seats. *syn.* leader

protection [prə·tek'shən] *n.* A
person or thing that
protects: The cave was our
protection from the storm.
syn. guard

Q

quietness [kwī'ət·nəs] *n.* The
state of having or making
very little noise: There was
nothing but *quietness* in the
house that night. *syns.*
silence, stillness

R

radio [rā'dē·ō] *n., pl.* **radios** A
machine that sends sounds
through the air from one
place to another. We heard
the new songs on our
radios. ■

realize [rē'əl·īz'] *v.* **realized,**
realizing To understand: I
realized that I had missed
dinner. *syn.* understand

reap [rēp] *v.* **reaped, reaping**
To bring in a crop: We
reaped the crops before the
rain started. *syns.* harvest,
gather

rear-wheel [rir'·(h)wēl'] *adj.*
Having to do with the back
wheel: The *rear-wheel* tire
was flat.

record [ri·kôrd'] **1** *v.* **recorded**
To put down for later use:
We *recorded* that song so we
can play it again. **2** *n., pl.*
recorder, recorders A
machine used to play back
things that have been
recorded: We took tape
recorders with us on our trip.

318

recognize [rek′əg·nīz′] *v.*
recognized, recognizing To
see someone or something
that is known: I will
recognize the right road when
we get there.

reflector [ri·flek′tər] *n.*
Something that catches and
shines back light that hits it:
We could see the boat when
our light shone on its
reflector. ■

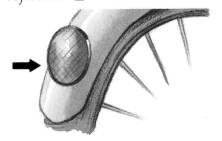

rehearsal [ri·hûr′səl] *n., pl.*
rehearsals A practice
performance: There was a
special *rehearsal* before the
play opened.

rehearse [ri·hûrs′] *v.*
rehearsed, rehearsing To
practice: The actors came to
rehearse for the play. *syn.*
practice

rhinoceros [rī·nos′ər·əs] *n., pl.*
rhinoceroses or **rhinoceros**
A large animal with a thick

skin and one or two horns:
The children ran to the pen
to look at the *rhinoceros.* ■

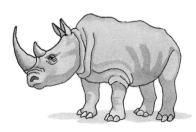

ride [rīd] *v.* **rode, ridden,
riding** To be carried on or
in: Have you ever *ridden* on
an elephant?

ruin [rōō′in] *n., pl.* **ruins**
What is left of something
that has been destroyed: We
saw the *ruins* of the old city
of Rome. *syn.* wreckage

S

---

safety [sāf′tē] *adj.* Free from
danger or harm: The driver
wore a *safety* belt.

a	add	o	odd	oi	oil
ā	ace	ō	open	ou	pout
â	care	ô	order	ng	ring
ä	palm	o͝o	took	th	thin
e	end	o͞o	pool	th	this
ē	equal	u	up	zh	vision
i	it	û	burn		
ī	ice	yo͞o	fuse		

ə = { a in *above* e in *sicken* i in *possible*
      o in *melon* u in *circus*

scenery [sē′nər·ē] *n.* Paintings used to make a stage look like some other place: The *scenery* in the play made the stage look like a haunted house.

sculpture [skulp′chər] *v.* To form by carving or shaping: The man will *sculpture* the statue. *syn.* carve

several [sev′ər·əl *or* sev′rəl] *adj.* More than two, but not many: We went away for *several* days.

shelter [shel′tər] *n.* Something that covers or protects: The deer looked for *shelter* in the forest. *syns.* housing, cover

siren [sī′rən] *n., pl.* **sirens** A device that makes a loud noise to warn people of danger: When the *siren* blew, we took cover in a safe place. *syn.* alarm ■

sketch [skech] **1** *n., pl.* **sketches** A rough, quickly done drawing: Your *sketch* of the house is very good. *syn.* drawing **2** *v.* **sketched, sketching** To make a sketch: Alexandra will *sketch* the trees. *syn.* draw

sportsmanship [spôrts′mən·ship′] *n.* Fair play in games: The players showed good *sportsmanship.*

sprocket [sprok′it] *n.* One of a number of teeth on a wheel: The *sprocket* broke off when he rode the bike up the hill.

squint [skwint] *v.* **squinted, squinting** She *squinted* when she first came out into the sun.

stroke [strōk] *n., pl.* **strokes** The breaking of a blood vessel in the brain: He was in bed for a long time after his *stroke.*

studio [st(y)o͞o′dē·ō] *n., pl.* **studios** A place to work or teach, as for an artist: She painted many pictures in her *studio. syns.* workshop, study

survive [sər·vīv′] *v.* **survived, surviving** To live through: The plants will *survive* the storm. *syns.* exist, outlive

---

T

---

tailor [tā′lər] *n., pl.* **tailors** A person who makes or fixes clothes: The *tailor* made a new coat for me.

tangle [tang′gəl] *v.* **tangled** To twist together: The ropes in the boat were *tangled. syn.* snarl

television [tel′ə·vizh′ən] *n.* The sending and receiving of pictures and sound by means of a special device: We saw the ball game on *television.*

texture [teks′chər] *n.* The look or feel of a surface: The *texture* of that table is smooth.

theater [thē′ə·tər] *n.* A place built for presentation of plays, films, and the like: We went to the *theater* to see the show.

thimble [thim′bəl] *n., pl.* **thimbles** A metal or plastic cap worn to protect the finger in sewing: I needed a new *thimble.* ■

thoughtful [thôt′fəl] *adj.* **thoughtfully** Full of thought: "It must have taken a lot of time to do that painting," the boy said *thoughtfully.*

thousand [thou′zənd] *n., pl.* **thousands** *adj.* Ten hundreds, written 1,000: Three *thousand* people watched the ball game.

a	add	o	odd	oi	oil
ā	ace	ō	open	ou	pout
â	care	ô	order	ng	ring
ä	palm	o͞o	took	th	thin
e	end	o͞o	pool	th	this
ē	equal	u	up	zh	vision
i	it	û	burn		
ī	ice	yo͞o	fuse		

ə = { a in *above*   e in *sicken*   i in *possible*
      { o in *melon*   u in *circus*

thread [thred] **1** *n., pl.* **threads** Thin silk or cotton used for sewing: He used red *thread* to sew his shirt. **2** *v.* **threaded, threading** To put through a needle: I couldn't see well, so Max *threaded* the needle for me.

throw [thrō] *v.* **threw, thrown, throwing** To make fly through the air: The ball was *thrown* high into the air. *syns.* fling, pitch

tighten [tīt'(ə)n] *v.* **tightened, tightening** To make tight or tighter: Sally's hand *tightened* on the handle.

tortoise [tôr'təs] *n., pl.* **tortoises** or **tortoise** A turtle, especially one that lives on land: The *tortoise* walked very slowly. *syn.* turtle

tower [tou'ər] *n., pl.* **towers** A tall, narrow building or part of a building: We could see the whole town from the library *tower.*

traffic [traf'ik] *n.* The number or movement of things or people passing along a route: The slow *traffic* made us late for the show.

type [tīp] *n., pl.* **types** A kind of things or people that have something in common: There are many *types* of houses. *syn.* kind

tumble [tum'bəl] *v.* **tumbled** To fall or cause to fall: The man did not see the toy on the sidewalk and *tumbled* down.

U

---

unicycle [yoō'nə·sī'kəl] *n., pl.* **unicycles** A vehicle with one wheel, a seat, and pedals: It is hard to ride a *unicycle.* ■

unload [un·lōd'] *v.* **unloaded** To empty things from: The movers *unloaded* the van. *syns.* dump, discharge

unpack [un·pak′] *v.* **unpacking**
To open and take out the
contents of: We were
unpacking the dishes from
the trunk. *syn.* open

unroll [un·rōl′] *v.* **unrolled** To
open out: We *unrolled* the
new rugs. *syns.* unfold,
unwind

untangle [un·tang′gəl] *v.*
untangled, untangling To
free from being tangled, or
snarled: Please help me
untangle this rope. *syns.*
unsnarl, unravel

usual [yōō′zhōō·əl] *adj.*
usually *adv.* In the common
or everyday way: We *usually*
leave a light on at night.
syn. normal

unusual [un·yōō′zhōō·əl] *adv.*
Not common: The clown
had a very *unusual* coat.
syns. rare, uncommon,
different

V

vacation [vā·kā′shən] *n., pl.*
vacations A time for rest
and fun, away from work or
school: Our *vacation* lasted
two weeks. *syn.* holiday

videotape [vid′ē·ō·tāp′] *n., pl.*
videotapes A kind of
magnetic tape used to record
television broadcasts: Alice
made some *videotapes* of the
shows.

W

weave [wēv] *v.* **wove, weaving**
To make something by
passing strips or threads
over and under one another:
Marissa *weaves* blankets and
rugs from yarn. *syns.* braid,
wind ■

a	add	o	odd	oi	oil
ā	ace	ō	open	ou	pout
â	care	ô	order	ng	ring
ä	palm	o͞o	took	th	thin
e	end	o͞o	pool	th	this
ē	equal	u	up	zh	vision
i	it	û	burn		
ī	ice	yo͞o	fuse		

ə = { a in *above*   e in *sicken*   i in *possible*
       o in *melon*   u in *circus* }

323

Word List

The following words are introduced in this book. Each is listed beside the number of the page on which it first appears.

Merle the High-Flying Squirrel
(6–15)

6 traffic
  frightened
7 quietness
8 realized
9 asleep
10 tangled
  untangle
  caught
  tumble
11 tightened
  whisper
12 whirlwind
  swirling
  powerful

Kites in Flight
(18–25)

18 thousand
  invent
20 usually
  materials
  cloth
21 types
  hundreds
22 flexi-kite
  novelty kite
23 flown

Bicycle Balloon Chase
(28–35)

28 bicycle
29 pedaled
  unicycle
30 aeronaut
  gondola
  unloaded
  unrolled

Diagrams
(36–39)

36 diagrams
37 labels
  inset
39 safety
  reflector
  rear-wheel
  sprocket

Bicycle Rider
(40–49)

41 several
42 handlebars
43 forty
44 half
  halfway
47 major
  fairness
  sportsmanship

Hilda, the Hen Who Wouldn't Give Up
(52–59)

52 hedge
53 helmets
54 engine
55 thrown
56 gently

Fantasy
(60–61)

61 exist

The Dragon of an Ordinary Family
(62–71)

62 ordinary
  fuddy-duddy
64 unusual
66 vacation
69 unpacking
  hopefully

Encore for Eleanor
(78–85)

78 encore
79 perform
80 sketch
  easel
  rhinoceros
  charcoal

Photographs

Key: (l) - Left; (r) - Right; (c) - Center; (t) - Top; (b) - Bottom.

Page 2, H. Zefa/H. Armstrong Roberts; 18, HBJ Photo; 19, Michael Pasdzior/The Image Bank; 20, HBJ Photo/Earl Kogler; 21 HBJ Photo/Earl Kogler; 22, HBJ Photo/Erik Arnesen; 73, David Muench; 88, Giraudon/Art Resource/Spaden; 91, Scala/Art Resource/Spaden; 93, Giraudon/Art Resource/Spaden; 110, BJ Photo; 113, HBJ Photo/Beverly Brosius; 122 (both), HBJ Photo; 136, David Muench/H. Armstrong Roberts; 141, H.G. Ross/H. Armstrong Roberts; 145, David Muench; 146, HBJ Photo; 147, HBJ Photo; 165, HBJ Photo; 166, HBJ Photo; 167 (both), HBJ Photo; 168, HBJ Photo; 169, HBJ Photo/Erik Arnesen; 175 (l), HBJ Photo/Erik Arnesen; 175 (r), HBJ Photo; 199, HBJ Trade Department; 201, Stu Perry/THE BURLINGTON FREE PRESS; 202, Peter Main/The Christian Science Monitor; 203, HBJ Photo; 217; HBJ Photo; 218, Ewing Galloway; 230, HBJ Photo/Rodney Jones; 231 (l), Museum of American Folk Art; 231 (r), Museum of American Folk Art; 232, Museum of American Folk Art; 235, HBJ Photo/Rodney Jones; 272 (tl), E.R. Degginger; 272 (lc) Richard C. Kerns; 272 (bl), James Kern; 272 (bc), E.R. Degginger; 272 (br) E.R. Degginger; 301, M Thonig/H. Armstrong Roberts.

Illustrators

Lynn Adams: 284–285; Don Almquist: 52–57; Shirley Breuel: 86–87, 119, 264–269; Jesse Clay: 152–159; David Cunningham: 40–47, 162–163; Dee Deloy: 150–151; Ted Enik: 114–118; Wayne Houis: 50–51; Laurie Johnson: 276–281; Pamela Johnson: 124–131; Gary Lippencott: 242–247; Charles McBarron: 23; Larry Mikec: 100–107; Dorothy Michelle Novick: 136–141, 262–263; David Rickman: 134–135; Steven Schindler: 252–259; Georgia Shola: 16–17; John Cover: Fred Marvin